THE LIVES OF THE POEMS

THE
BAGLEY
WRIGHT
LECTURE
SERIES

JOSHUA BECKMAN

THE LIVES OF THE POEMS

WAVE BOOKS

SEATTLE AND NEW YORK

Published by Wave Books

www.wavepoetry.com

Wave Books titles are distributed to the trade by

Consortium Book Sales and Distribution

Phone: 800-283-3572 / SAN 631-760X

Library of Congress Cataloging-in-Publication Data

Names: Beckman, Joshua, 1971– author.

Title: The lives of the poems and three talks / Joshua Beckman.

Description: Seattle : Wave Books, [2018]

Identifiers: LCCN 2017001232 |

ISBN 9781940696423 (trade paperback)

Classification: LCC PS3552.E2839 A6 2017 | DDC 811/.54—dc23

LC record available at https://lccn.loc.gov/2017001232

Designed by Quemadura

Printed in the United States of America

9 8 7 6 5 4 3 2 1

First Edition

THE LIVES OF THE POEMS

INTRODUCTION

I gave this talk three times and am presenting here each of the three basically unedited. I had initially intended to write a single talk that could be given many times (each time using different poems as examples). The thought, I guess, was to create something that explained the experience of making the poems and allowed individual poems to float comfortably inside that presented experience. My sense was not that the poems were interchangeable, but just that they had come to be in similar ways, that whatever could be said about them, whatever helpful contextualizing and explaining, was somehow less varied than the poems themselves. So after giving the first, I traveled three thousand miles to give the second. But by the time I got there I had changed not only all of the poems, but much of the prose as well. Each new poem seemed to unhinge or alter its explanation, and the similarity of their circumstances became less interesting and recognizable than the slight changes each poem provoked. And by the time I was done with the third, the same sort of thing had happened, with really only the beginning, end, and basic architecture staying intact. Here are all three typed up from notes. The improvisational parts I have left untranscribed, and because much of the presentation hinged on the physical presence of my notebooks and drafts I have included images of them throughout.

THE LIVES OF THE POEMS

[SPOKANE–JANUARY 27, 2014]

This lecture is called THE LIVES OF THE POEMS & what I would like to talk with you about today are some poems I wrote between 2009 and 2013 – I want to introduce you to them, I want to talk with you about my experience of making them, their experience of being made, our experience of living together – how it all came to happen and of their lives and experiences since that time.

Yesterday, sitting in a cafe in downtown Spokane working on this talk with little piles of poems spread out on my table – the waitress walked by – she said without even slowing a bit for an answer, "haiku?" – so I should say, my answer, the one that almost came out of me was yes – not exactly because I think of them as haiku, or not at all because I think of them as haiku, but because I think of haiku – because the experience of making haiku of reading haiku is important to me – one I'm close to – the experience of the haiku poet as itinerant, and the experience of the haiku poet as daily practitioner – the constant presence of the poem – the poetry – that it can happen at any time – that it can happen in any place –

I met a haiku poet once and I didn't know any Japanese and he didn't know any English and we couldn't have been together five minutes before I pulled out my notebook to write something down and he started smiling and pulled out a very similar one to show me – and from that point on (and maybe before that point without us knowing it) we were writing poems together – and the experience of haiku – its history is a collaborative one – it began as a collaborative form of longer linked parts that demanded a social practice, and even after it became the way we now commonly think of it, it maintained at its core a practice of sharing – of sharing one's own and others' together – of traveling and making with other poets – the experience is less isolated than most other writing practices – the number – the quantity – the constancy of presence in the life of the haiku poet of the poem of poetry – Takuboku (a tanka poet) wrote more than 10,000 poems before he died at the age of twenty-seven – and most haiku poets would write thousands over a lifetime – and what is important about this is the necessary relation such a process has to the poet's daily life – saturated – and think how such a practice allows for the presence of language in its fragmentary vibrancy – a constant – (Okay, I should read you some of my poems now so you hear them) –

cloth
on line
and line from tree
on earth

limb shadow
silhouettes entertaining us
as we live

■

want
so strange
and big
in scape of
empty sky
(cut out)
moon-black pillars
resisting
opaque time

There is something inherently indiscreet about a meaningful poem – the poem, its capabilities in flux – the poet and the reader in flux – so that each encounter (as with a person) is different – even if in most ways (as with a person) it is familiar – and some would say the same thing about the other arts – and I'm talking – I'm thinking – about poetry – but just because something is the manifestation of the real peculiarities of something, it doesn't mean the same thing can't be the manifestation of the peculiarities of something else – no real actuality in art negates another – like people –

on my
lips smashed
where the wet rocks
make moss

up from life
we spire in light

so the physical experience – the growing moving language – inside outside of me – ends up in this notebook – or starts in this notebook – or

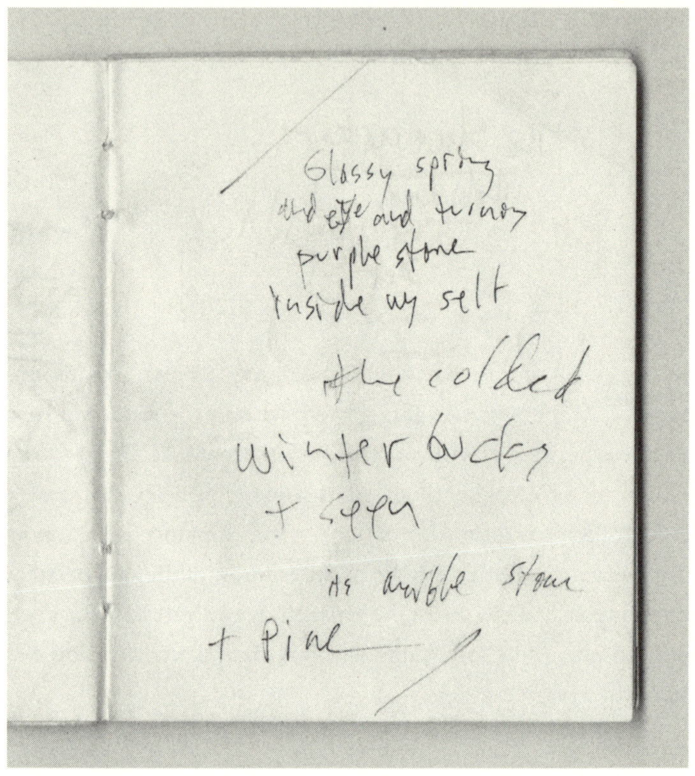

first when it appears as words, as written words, appears in this notebook – and that has been the case for nearly all of my poems for many years – but now let me show you a little pile of papers and talk about *how* these poems were made –

[talk about paper, typing & white out, carrying them around / place, the physical making / a relation to each other]

atoms made
scandelous and
dropy/in ~~presence~~
~~of~~ bright
open ~~flower~~ presence
of me
my portait's
a cup

Sky
not some
cold rainy thing
but blue before
and turned away

A frozen gush
my fever

now full leaked
of summer

and some few had titles which would exist as underlining some word or group of words inside the poem – so the title might appear where it was found –

mountain's
silver side
by wind
in wind to shape
of winter
orchard
birds
hopping about
for nothing
beneath it
its shadow

and there were certain other organic innovations – and when I say that, I only mean innovations for us – me and the poems – everything's been done – everything's been tried – and that's not a challenge it's a liberty

– so that when those innovations sprouted they would get the rest of the poem messy with possibility – and sometimes I would see it and sometimes I wouldn't see it till later – & when I recognized them – when I recognized those innovations – it helped me see in ways where my human energies were – I would identify the time or place – they were abstract but they were very physical and real to me and I didn't want to separate from them – I didn't want to separate from the physical experience of writing them – so when a date appeared in the middle of a poem –

sunflowers
(September 17)
dead now
with sparrows on them
light
yellow
and pale
pulling something
with its mouth

the date is inside the poem and parenthetical and here a dedication the same –

sick
hurt
breaths
(For T)
gasping
and breathing
and falling
and fear

Somehow I think the physical presences and constructive impulses are exposed – you recognize or feel the madeness – the oscillation of feeling and effect – as the balance of something coming into view – its recognition and surprise – there's no purchase on it – it is spans of time reanimated – various particles of meaning constituting temporarily – the coming together of the organic infinite – that thing which disallows a real inquirer from accepting finite boundaries – you see the cloud you see it there you enjoy its form – you accept the unequivocal temporariness of it – and I want for a moment you to think of the poem as a temporary accumulation of resonances – and the poem in time the way music is in time – basically there when it is happening and not when it is not – not like a painting, which feels as if it's making the same damn face whether the Louvre is open or closed – but like music – and the text is a score and the poem is that thing that happens when you animate it –

this head it hangs me up
like stoic falsish stones
that stare at walls
they prop
and fall
to sleep
for countless years
its iced-up roof
its planked and diamond
boards its twisted
guts of ashy smoke

■

rips and passions
thrust at least
I smell
cause all alone
and smelling
here I lie
no drunken pulse
to drudge on up
or sigh, I lived
a simple life
described behind my back
as swat and fly

You hear the rhyme going on in these – some started short and felt like loops – the process of them seemed to be a smoothing down – like a rock tumbler – reading them over & over again – making slight changes until they were smooth – until I heard them smooth –

as if in sleep
the ocean's homely wheeze
had ceased
I dreamed
and felt myself
increased

and that is the most microcosmic version of sanding down – but there are bigger poems that had the same sort of movement to them – that had the same kind of experience – to be said over & over again – to be heard – to be aloud – and that kind of language making of language forming encourages, at least in me, a movement toward rhyme –

hummed up mouths
when the lights are out
our bodies wandering
in a field around

goslings gently
growing in nests
their soft fur wings
in
sense
they called
with their little cries
like static on
those telephones at times
and inside the mind
there live events of sky

and some were bigger and more unwieldy but still found themselves holding together through the magnetic tension of rhyme – creating loops & loops – loops in loops – bigger circles – and they were encouraging of each other – a line and a sound would echo – and from that resonance a poem would appear – and from that poem the reading and reading it the hearing and hearing it – some triggering sound my body would respond to with reply –

circle flowers
giving up and gone
made a circle of
my own soft one
then earth water
water sun, for you
I thought, you're coming home

one of the pleasures – maybe one of the worrisome pleasures of rhyme is its ability to suspend – to allow an ungrounding of sense or meaning until one has comfortably arrived at the end of the line, the rhyme – so the experience of these was that they encouraged each other – that they multiplied, that within them loops and turns grow dynamically extending – within the poems that suspension – and even at times with such extended release it became all that –

seasons clinging
to steam my art
this month this year's a light
beam like what silver thins out
to expose a tree
dust
lean
foss
swee

but when I think of the lives of these poems – these rhyming ones in particular – there was a time when they had to be put away – to be taken away from the others – and the real others I'm thinking about here are the future others – because they had moved me – my body – into a responsive abstraction of sound – and everything that got started would instantly circle back on itself – so I couldn't read them anymore – I put them away – and started again – again and again this attempted being present making presence – putting some away – holding others –

And it was probably around then that I started trying to think of all these poems as a book – or at least tried to move them around – tried to find some form for them – I remember I was giving a reading at a friend's place and in getting ready for that tried to construct, to formulate, something about them – and ended up splitting them into regions – while writing them I lived in New York and Seattle – and went often to friends in California – so the poems from New York in New York, Seattle Seattle – the poems from the desert, calling them The Desert or California – and the poems sort of contorted to fit – even a poem obviously and comfortably located in the desert is strangely altered by having the word *desert* before it – and having a group of other poems sharing the location – and the strange reality of locating the other places – New York and Seattle – so that when a poem had mountains it was certainly Seattle but it could also oddly be New York thinking of Seattle –

These poems all traveled back and forth with me for years and it maybe strikes one as odd but even the slightest shifts in language register – a line break or change becomes an invisible notched marking (memoried) – so that some impulse, some energy is from a different place – and much of the impulse to note place at all was about a kind of truthful human presence and grounding – so that eventually the fact of their itinerancy made it too uncomfortable (for me) to designate them this way – and it took months for them to shake back out and seem next to one another untethered by their locales – and still the desert ones in particular resisted – and at times I attribute it to the peculiarities of the landscape – its sparseness and the immediate difference of the material world as it appears in the poems – but it seems to me now like it is something more about the attention – the quiet – the solitary tone – even when Anthony and Kirsty show up –

Dust brushed
again by wind
some miles away

the optic scene
like steam
a sun
going down presents itself
as up

and I'm out here
watching it do that

(October 28, 2011
Joshua Tree, California
just after 5:30)

and Anthony and Kirsty
on their way

I was saying I didn't want to separate from the physical experience of writing them, of them coming to be, and that became more and more clear as I shared them with others – I started to give readings – I started to talk about the poems – and my experience of those readings was disconcerting – I found the bigger the audience the less appealing the experience and that the poems seemed to dissipate in air – they could not project out into an audience – you see, they want to be aloud but they need intimacy and concentration – the experience of them is meditative on both sides of the poem – is meditative and quiet – so that presenting them with force almost shatters them before they get to the listener –

I found myself compelled to turn down large readings and accept small ones and the more I did them the smaller and smaller they became – until a gallery in Los Angeles invited me to read and we decided to post a schedule for private one-on-one readings – each a half hour long – all day – you would sign up for a time and come sit with me and we would sit there and I would read – well, at some point an acquaintance arrived and I said what I would like, what I would really like is to have you read to me – read my poems to me – and so we sat there for half an hour and she read the entire stack of them –

So these poems want to be read aloud – they want to be read to others – they want privacy and intimacy – they function, they thrive in shared loving sound – they do not force the disinterested – they are dead to the skeptical – they are even, in their most abstract, exceptionally personal – and I found myself wanting to talk about them, wanting to be able to talk about them –

When people ask what your poems are like it's like asking – it's confusing and overwhelming and it's easy to, out of a desire not to be reductive – to flail and not really answer – but I found I really wanted to answer – I found the poems were so present I really needed to answer – and I had some poems that felt like they became for me the answer –

made poems
from actual things
shadow falling
wall black wings
of blackbird flap
on bunch of
big dry straw
like a play

■

and now
as through
an oval frame
morning light
appears on everything
to shine

light bits of presence – experienced experience – sometimes I said they were like abstract still lifes of moments of sunlight – the gleams – the reflection – and those poems started to feel like the center of the body of work – they were helping me and others know the work – and these two –

cloud on
cloud top now
above the actual
town
mountains

pooled-up water
where people
sometimes swim

▪

Dial of landscape

volcanoes covered with snow
blue lakes inside of them
inside of them

they call crystal

Well those two – while I lived in Seattle and looked at the mountains and thought about the alpine lakes and thought about the alpine flowers their isolation and delicacy – the care – their vibrancy – these had always been in the pile – they always had the others constellating around them – and so for me these were in a real way – they are – they remain – the most meaningful the most important of the poems – but none of these poems – none of the ones you heard this afternoon are actually in the book I published – I wrote hundreds and hundreds of poems – and then I made a book – which is something else – something exciting and real – but something else – and the lives of these poems are just different – not better or worse, not something more or less successful – their lives just continue in a more or less private fashion – except, I guess, for times like this.

THE LIVES OF THE POEMS

[NEW YORK–MAY 8, 2014]

What I would like to talk with you about today are some poems I wrote between 2008 and 2012 – I want to introduce you to them, I want to talk with you about my experience of making them, their experience of being made, our experience of living together – how it all came to happen and of their lives and the experiences since that time –

I was sitting in a cafe working on this talk with little piles of poems spread out on my table – the waitress walked by and said without even slowing a bit for an answer, "haiku?" – so I should say, my answer, the one that almost came out of me – was yes – not exactly because I think of them as haiku, or not at all because I think of them as haiku, but because I think of haiku – because the experience of making haiku of reading haiku is important to me – one I'm close to – the experience of the haiku poet as itinerant and the experience of the haiku poet as daily practitioner – the constant presence of the poem – the poetry – that it can happen at any time – that it can happen in any place –

I met a haiku poet once and I didn't know any Japanese and he didn't know any English and we couldn't have been together five minutes before I pulled out my notebook to write something down and he started smiling and pulled out a very similar one to show me – and from that point on (and really before that point without us knowing it) we were writing poems together – and the experience of haiku – its history is a collaborative one – it began as a collaborative form of longer linked parts that demanded a social practice, and even after it came to be the way we now commonly think of it, it maintained at its core a practice of sharing – of sharing one's own and others' together – of traveling and making with other poets – the experience is less isolated than most other writing practices – the number the quantity – the constancy of presence in the life of the haiku poet, of the poem, of poetry – a haiku poet would write easily thousands of poems in even a short lifetime – and what is important about this is the necessary relation such a process has to the poet's daily life – its saturated qualities – and think how such a practice allows for the presence of language in its fragmentary vibrancy – a constant realizing of the world in language – but I want to read you some of my poems now so you hear them –

Grey as is
  the counseled star
in little strips

    my shoulders ache
and my body
having gotten water
still needs more

■

  poppy fields
through Peter's window
      dried

grasping

for trash

and de-populate

I stare

So I want to show you some things and talk about the physical experience of these poems – the growing moving language – inside outside of me – ends up in this notebook – or first when it appears as words as written words appears in this notebook – and that has been the case for nearly all of my poems for many years – now let me show you a little pile of papers – and talk about *how* these poems were made –

in eyes
blue seed
lights and crowns
in beak
also rainday crashing
on the window
~~with a nothing~~
spring frames
of glass
knocked back
~~by wind~~

ligh

[TALK ABOUT 1. PAPER DIMENSIONS 2. TYPING & WHITE OUT 3. CARRYING THEM AROUND / PLACE 4. THE PHYSICAL MAKING A RELATION TO EACH OTHER / ROCK TUMBLER]

Head leaf
big green & I
hear music

from a hollow box
in a peace-filled bubble

that was itself kind of there
and like the earth

the poem – its capabilities in flux – the poet and the reader in flux – so that each encounter (as with a person) is different – even if in most ways (as with a person) it is familiar – you listen to it & you speak it –

distant I, I drawn
in smoking puffs
to end in loops
like puffs
right up.

Up to the sun?

Yes, up.

■

told stole pill
pushing into the sleeping swallow's
throat dissolved

a bluish sheen and a simple
perfect entrance opened in a hill

The magnetic relation of poems to each other – them shifting – tugging – pulling each other into or out of alignment – and it is less mystical than it sounds – if I have a pile of small poems – go through it – read it – listen – and it is not the moment of any one thing – poem – but a shared momentum or relation – the relational push and pull – as parts of one thing – no, not really that – you hear a sound – you hear a sound repeated – in feeling those things – sometimes recognized – your relation to both is changed – and theirs to each other – in being recognized but just in being, too – you are writing moving listening your way through – it's how the poems get made – as you bring new poems into their space – as new poems are there beside them – being read – time – and each new relation with each new neighbor poem – maybe that's the tumbling – and the forming – so separate it seems at moments it can exist – which maybe is only that reading impulse – to return to the beginning of the poem – not to be removed – not to be removed from the others & on its own – but that way of not being done that sends you back in by way of the beginning – or any other place for that matter – being aloud and together provoking a kind of batted-around echo in the world – and it is locating, temporary and eventual – and while this moving back and forth was happening – this kind of toggling – changing or not changing – each poem would almost responsively solidify between its neighbors – and moved it might do it some more – until that solid-

up ~~dear~~ all ~~up~~
~~on~~ giant morning
up as your voice
rolls in big
~~and fat~~
~~like a~~ lonely
fearful will
now fearless
in its open field
so spherical
and yours.

ifying became real – a responding – and that solidifying was for me – so that then I was – in a way – done with it – or done with it for then – and I could just blow through it with my voice – the other kind of making, that is changing, put away –

night

huddled memory
of back throbbing bone

this pill

some flesh
some skin on it

▪

wisely locust dull
and dreary knocking
about beneath the
cleared-out moon

(light from sixes)

Understanding the poem – there is a kind of death imposed on the poem by those who try and understand it completely – even just the understanding impulse includes some desire to be done – some desire to complete the experience – that one might get on to new experiences – new poems – but there is something inherently indiscreet about a meaningful poem – it is in yourself or someone else or the world making meaning, and meaningful things are always in motion – by the very nature of us (people) finding them that way –

grain that's skinny
on its stalk and thought too
conversing vertically
like fumes

    the way you say
of a hidden bird
its song, then
stick your hand out
palm & crumb

At some point I should say I don't want to be done with the poems – I'm in no hurry to be done – maybe that's clear – I enjoy the thought that others are reading them privately – that others are sharing them – that they are playing some role in others' lives – but then they are away – and so for me there is no rush in that direction – the experience at that point becomes diffuse – maybe it is the interrelatedness – the interconnectedness – and it is almost too concrete to say that they are left together because they might – any one or part might still influence any other one or part – it's too practical – there are times when you prune a plant for its own good – and times when you make cuttings – it's less a metaphor than a way – I am guided as a person by the growths and tendings of plants – the relations – the awareness of organic things that are one more than one and part of one all at once –

Little house and
            window duh
                        circledup
            kinda dumb
                the light's not

on or gone
just waiting for the coming sun
like cactus flowers
longing some
I'm thinking of that orange one
opened up in only form
simple form of bowl or drum
then falling flat
on table done

It feels like if there is some – any – possibility for change – any relating to it as writing – the process of writing – that reading it over is certainly writing – a kind of writing – even not looking not listening feels like a kind of writing – there in its pile left with the others and its potential – and that waiting still might be writing if you return to it – even if you don't – ravenous or disinterested – it is easy to imagine putting poems away as letting them settle – settle into themselves – so they can be returned to and seen clearly – but just as likely their mess takes over – they start to grow together or mold – a kind of compost that leaving alone making becomes –

It's strange – as I started to look around I found groups of poems put away everywhere – they had been going through these cycles – had basically been off on their own (I still find them – I found a small batch this week working on the talk) – and even just to prepare for this new encounter is a kind of writing of them I guess –

my guts
my ribs
my skin

I'm in this cold air
  this city this room
  and over this body

    I stink like some
    sweet fermenting thing

  still with my mind
 I call you up

it seems private now reading it, and so hid away feels right – I didn't even realize it was happening – a friend said what about those other ones I saw – and I went looking for them – and then I found them – grouped together, about forty real short ones like –

bee bee buzzing
over puff dead clover flower

wrapped together and tucked away as if on some trip – from some trip – not that they were over – but that their togetherness needed to be maintained – so much time went by – that they had been – felt present – some I'd even notice in others –

like a place
that's gone rubbed down

you can't see it but they are similar even in how they look – where the words are and how they're acting – I'm not sure how to explain it – but putting them away – at times – felt more like sharing them – or maybe it was the me of then staying with them in some way – while the me of now moved on – and I like sharing them – sometimes sharing them privately – there was a Jane Freilicher show & I made some poems – I think the space of making the poems I was making made a space for making poems everywhere – some space of being in the presence of poems differently – they were barely there as things – slight and gestural – that I could be on some porch by the water – which I couldn't – but I could do this – I could do this all the time if I wanted –

put in a bright blue cup
beside the world

▪

it's a mess
where I keep my flowers
living, half-living
by a window
last summer

and I kept thinking I'd send them to her – which I wouldn't – and so they would find themselves in letters together – in and out – imagined and real – kinda packed and ready to go –

yellow was the color
and I felt falling
on myself its symbols

and this was the one I returned to the most – it shining a light on the other poems later – they were growing privately – or off in actual letters – on their way to live with individual others – I liked this one a lot and shared it with a friend –

rosemary flowering
in this week's now

while I was out of town
    you were in my house
you were walking around

and that is how I read it – and she read it like this, the *you were*'s a bit more accusatory –

rosemary flowering
in this week's now
  while I was out of town
    you were in my house
you were walking around

which cracked me up – and one new affect for the poem appears – its capability – its vagueness is basically the deal it made with us so we could share it – and so in reading them in trying to inhabit them – we move around – I think it's why I feel like it's still writing – like the language – it's changing – the people keep changing – and the private experience expands – its repetition – but not just its repetition – its ways – I was working with Jon on a book – we were looking at poems and listening to them – but we were wanting them to share with others – that's another side of it – and there – there's a poem he is in – its underlined title – I think of – the qualities of that line – those thin strips of metal that make it – you set a poem out – and print it – you leave it there in lead – but I assume we carry it around with us – set – while countless other words fly around doing their business all the time – doing whatever things they do – not really right here in front of us at all – but set in print and shared – it's still a private thing – books and their private experience – being in people's lives – over time – entering – returning

The Letteropener

Jon says peculiar
is my heart, resolute
is my soul

the world around
does rest or freak

but I stay
quietly here
and reside,

see.

to – being lived with – shared – made private, almost singular – and in relation to you – being physical things – Bashō used to slip a poem into the conversation and if it went unnoticed it was a success – I think of those and the unsuccessful ones, too – never even getting written down – just awkwardly remaining a part of the conversation – and some poems find the outward quality of a private experience fulfills in all ways their outward needs – love poems can do this simply by being given – or the poem you kept reading all winter – meaning all *that* winter & not this – or writing – imagine an occasional poem unwittingly making it so – and making the occasion along with it – and they're lost as many little private gifts – like breath – still entering the air – ephemeral and real –

joy in dusted
selves made small
the tender bean of lea
and growing
flopping leaf

(then little me)

to crescent lake
went green and blue
on paths of moss
then looked and saw
the mouths I passed

this one's called Kitty's Pregnant –

the earth
has on its airs and gasses
plants and trees

Kitty's pregnant

so I feel
myself as if I'm
living with other people
moans and spurs
of intimate feeling
sitting there with it
in my room

the title just right there in the middle and I underlined it – as I write or once I know it's there and there it stays –

atoms made
scandalous
and droppy
in bright open presence
of me
my portrait's
a cup

Sometimes they'd be there resisting the rest – creating some space – here – inside sound – and there were other organic innovations – and when I say that I only mean for us – me and the poems – everything's been done – everything's been tried – and that's not a challenge it's a liberty – so that when those innovations appeared they would get the rest of the poems shaken up with possibility – and sometimes I would see it and sometimes I wouldn't see it till later – and when I would recognize them it helped me see in ways where my human energies were – I would identify the time or place in a poem – physical and real to me – and I didn't want to separate from it – so a date and place would be there – in the middle – like the titles as if recognized – the physical presence and the constructive impulses – exposed and reoccurring – dates and times and places in parentheses – and dedications appear in the same way too –

Dust drills
and absent
light

How will I be
and where, cries
(for Mr. Creeley)
the me.

something about allowing those things that might otherwise begin or end a poem to be inside allows for more fluidity – it makes them all-around – partial – relational –

sail of light sun's lope
it's all to say of things
my mind here set –

brick built arch
around me air

Listen and this oscillation of feeling and effect – as the balance of something coming into view – its recognition and surprise – there's no pur-

~~a~~ fire
for each cloud
head griefy and still
~~on the~~ ends of
~~that~~ tree ~~stick~~
waiting ~~to~~
grow

a fire
for each cloud
head griefy
and still
ends of trees
waiting
grow

chase on it – it is spans of time reanimated – vaporous particles of meaning constituting temporarily – the coming together of the organic infinite – that thing which disallows a real inquirer from accepting finite boundaries – you see the cloud you see it there you enjoy its form – you accept the unequivocal temporariness of it – and I want for a moment – you to think for a moment of the poems as a temporary accumulation of resonances – and the poem in time the way music is in time – basically there when it is happening – and the text is a score and the poem is that thing that happens when you animate it – the poem is the unassessable accumulation of those animations –

Blake's case was
being made, loud voices
clapped at us and went away
I sat with my coffee
considering what to say
and then it came
as a day beside a day
I write it down, and look:

look how the light
on that wall stays

Some started short and felt like loops – the process of them seemed to be a smoothing down – reading them over and over again – tapping at them slightly – until I heard them –

Leaves too
shaking
and playing, getting
shook, I hear outside the

land storm now
I've gone to bed
the shaking
windows
as a thing have ceased to shake
while I am here, a partial
body in the lake

to be said over & over – to be heard – to be aloud – and that kind of language making – language forming, encourages, in me a movement toward rhyme –

It's winter
and the cliffy halves
of sun sure themselves
on building clouds
and make their forms

I made a home
of wistful hoots
the weather let me do it too
now I'll watch
the storm move through

eyes ungloomed
and I'm here too
where
the grasses boom
yellow grasses
iced-up soon
blackbirds,
cue

Held together by that magnetic tension of rhyme – creating loops in loops – and they were encouraging of each other – a line a sound would echo – and from that resonance a poem would appear – and from that poem the reading and reading it the hearing and hearing it – some triggering sound my body would respond to with reply –

light's out
steam and being lit
my place
was pink and grey
I sat down to watch
and as with day day's passing
came a dark blanket
silver of late

▪

river's taken space was made
and apple-eaters framed
by glassy straights
and floppy falls of late
an icy spray sort of white and grey
then claims and praise
sunlight's solid state was play
in the high part of the day

I stayed, my train
at Croton-Harmon got delayed
but that's okay

It started to feel like too much – these rhyming ones in particular – there was a time when they had to be put away – from the others – the future others – because they had moved me – my body – into a responsive procession of sound – and everything that got started would instantly circle back on itself – so I couldn't read them anymore – I put them away – and started again – again and again this attempted being present making presence – putting some away – holding others –

I remember I was giving a reading and in getting ready for that tried to construct – to formulate something about the poems – and ended up splitting them into regions – poems from New York, from Seattle – the poems from the desert, calling them The Desert or California – and the poems sort of contorted to fit – even a poem obviously and comfortably located in the city is strangely altered by having the name of its city before it – and having a group of other poems sharing its location – and the strange reality of locating the other places – a bus could be in two cities at once, or neither.

These poems all traveled back and forth with me for years and it maybe strikes one as odd but even the slightest shifts in language register – a line break or change becomes an invisible notched marking – so that some impulse some energy is from a different place – and much of that impulse to note place at all was about a kind of truthful human presence and grounding – so that eventually the fact of their basic itinerancy made it too uncomfortable (for me) to designate them this way – and it took months for them to shake back out and seem next to one another untethered by their locale –

new fable of
little yellow mouth
opens up on window

grasping lots
and waving fragrant plumes

I most lonely have been
everywhere walking streets
and island water drops in eye

■

Left my house in little spring
with knits of holes
and apples hanging there
upon the tree wood tack and note
snow ice and solid white on lake
then coming up like simple dreams

it's summer's
refreshing rain dripped
in a pot in my mind
and a yard and a sun
and a rosewood plank
so big I'd lie down
and spread out all my stuff

I was saying I didn't want to separate from the physical experiences of writing them – of them coming to be – and that became more and more clear as I shared them with others – I started to give readings – I started to talk about the poems – and my experience of those readings was disconcerting –

I found the bigger the audience the less appealing the experiences and that the poems seemed to dissipate in air – they could not project out into an audience – they needed an intimacy and a concentration – the experience of them is meditative on both sides of a reading – is meditative and quiet – so that presenting them with force almost shatters them before they get to the listener –

I found myself giving smaller and smaller readings, and the more I did them the smaller they became – until a friend in Los Angeles invited me – and we decided to post a schedule for one-on-one readings – each a half hour long – all day – you would sign up for a time and come sit with me and we would sit there and I would read – well, at some point an acquaintance arrived and I realized what I would like what I would really like is to have her read to me – read my poems to me – and so we sat there for half an hour and she read the entire stack of them – each quietly to herself and then aloud to me and I realized, yes, these poems want to be read aloud –

I was hearing them – they want to be read to others but they want a privacy and intimacy – they function they thrive in shared loving sound – they do not force the disinterested – they are dead to the skeptical – they are even, in their most abstract, exceptionally personal – and I found myself wanting to talk about them wanting to be able to talk about them – when people ask what your poems are about it's confusing and overwhelming and it's easy, out of a desire not to be reductive, to flail and not really answer – but I found I really wanted to answer – I found that some poems were so present they were showing themselves as obvious answers –

this week I drew with silver
a perfect shiny circle

that lay in the garden's center
like a pool
for the flowers to stare at

▪

shadows falling
black
of blackbird flap
on bunch of
big dry straw
like a play

Light bits of presence – experienced experience – sometimes I said they were like abstract still lifes of moments of sunlight – the gleams – the reflection – and those poems started to feel like the center of the work – they were helping me and others know the work – and of other times – there they were – looking at me – asking me – more body than anything –

out gulls now
designed like
snow in mouth
of hollow rock
blown round

and those had always been in the pile – with others constellating around them – and so for me these were in a real way – they are – they remain – at some center of things – but none of these poems – none of the ones you heard this afternoon – are actually in the book I read to everyone yesterday – I wrote hundreds and hundreds of poems – also, I made that book – which is something else – and the lives of these poems are just different – not better – not worse – not something more or less successful – their lives just continued in a more private fashion – except for maybe times like this – when they poke out their heads and say hello.

THE LIVES OF THE POEMS

[TUCSON–SEPTEMBER 11, 2014]

What I'd like to do today is introduce you to some poems – tell you about their lives – experiences – and ways – I would like to tell you about my life with them – our lives together – the social spaces we occupy and share – and to some extent, I hope, how we have come to be the ways we are –

I was working on this pile of poems – spread out on my table – at a coffee shop – the waitress walked by – she said – without even slowing for an answer – "haiku?" – so I should say – my answer – the one that almost came out of me was yes – not exactly because I think of them as haiku – or not at all because I think of them as haiku – but because there is something in the experience of making haiku of reading haiku that is important to me – a way I'm close to – the experience of the haiku poet as itinerant – traveling and making a kind of document – time and movement – and the experience of the haiku poet as daily practitioner – the moments – all of them – the small scales of time – the spaces they make – the constant presence of the poem – the poetry – in the world, the world in it – that it can happen at any time – that it can happen in any place –

I met a haiku poet once and I didn't know any Japanese and he didn't know any English and we couldn't have been together five minutes before I pulled out my notebook to write something down and he started smiling and pulled a very similar one out to show me – and from that point on (and really before that point without us knowing it) we were writing poems together – and the experience of haiku – its history is a collaborative one –

It began as a collaborative form of longer linked parts that demanded a social practice, and even after it came to be the way we now commonly think of it, it maintained at its core a practice of sharing – of sharing one's own and others' together – of traveling and making with other poets – the number the quantity – the constancy of presence in the life of the haiku poet of the poem of poetry – the haiku poet would write easily thousands of poems in even a short life – and what is important about this is the necessary relation such a process has to the poet's daily existence – its saturating qualities – poetry passing in and out of you – think how such a practice allows for the presence of language in its fragmentary vibrancy – think how the imaginations and things of the world are activated – that constant releasing of the world in language – ways that can come to have a gestural quality – witnessed iterated felt – resolving necessarily and somewhat immediately into other movements – and that happening all the time –

I want you to imagine a poem – an individual poem – as part of some greater span of poetry – like a shock from some expanse of energy – static and flash from the living world –

ashy cataracts
plastered as a sign
on my just got up why

■

balanced
lazing like
with me

and sunshine
on the street

so the life is to exist and integrate as thoroughly as possible into that existence the poetic act – it's the becoming – all the ways of being in the world are its way through its way – that it is the space through which the senses and intelligences pass – but saying that is already too outside – a kind of breathing metabolism – social and private – bodily and immersive – porous – not controlled and exhibited – part of – physical – and made –

gush
of sun
my body's
blood

spring's red beads
and winter done

We so often connect haiku with the natural world – but I end up thinking of the street photographers of the '60s and '70s – walking around and immersed in constant responsive construction – I think of Garry Winogrand, who said he photographed to see what things look like photographed – but was only telling half the truth – when he died there were 2,000 rolls of undeveloped film in his apartment – it seems maybe he photographed to be photographing –

Parasol of
dust goes poof

          and here
come the green
weeds, up the
brick wall again

So I want to show you some things and read you some things and talk about the physical experiences of these poems – how they appear and are formed – how they change and grow – the space in time they get made and how on the page they live – beside each other with each other – and me inside outside me – this notebook is where I see them first – where I write them down – and there and then an ink and paper thing of them is made – this book that's always with me – I made this book, too – paper folded and sewn and put in my pocket and walked around with always – so always or almost always when a poem appears for me, this is where it appears –

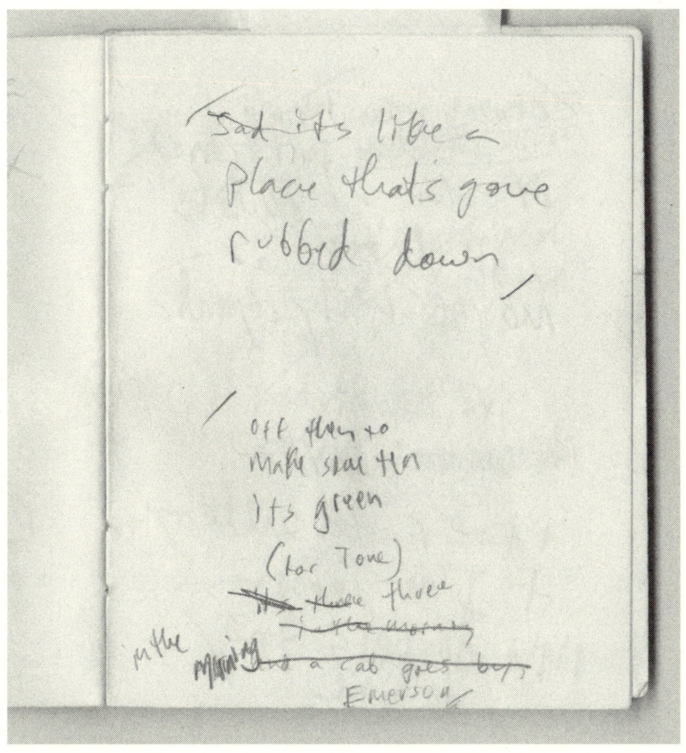

so there it is and I keep carrying it around – or soon others or other things of life appear beside it – above it on top of it – and around with me it goes – and these poems – the ones I'm talking about today – I would go home and there I had a pile of paper like this – this is actually some of it – cut down to a bit bigger than five by seven inches – I don't know why – I just wanted some small space for each poem – waiting – there the empty pile – and easy to throw into my typewriter and type one up –

Popped little
mary dahlia
into the mouth
of a cold day

and a spider's
straight web
flying over a
grass field
detached

hard

rudely grossly

to the earth

falls the flower

with its color

its tender fragile

body on the

stone floor, pink

on the grey floor

stone

– and then sit with a pile of them all together – shuffle through and read – and always I would have a pen or some white out and sort of scratch them down or build them up a bit – made things – messing with them – and as the pile grows and gets made – gets bigger – the poems could rub down to nothing – I had a kind of perverse relation to the white out – knowing that once gone – soon forgotten – soon forgotten and really gone – it was this making space – a kind of porous relation to the physical thing that had appeared – I could then write over where the white was some totally different word – or leave the space there as air or time to be seen or heard as empty space is heard – and I could hold the little batch of poems – I could hold a hundred or two hundred in a bag easy and then go off wherever I was off to – so I found that they, in all the traveling we actually did, would get shuffled and shook – would get constantly read aloud when carried around – and so one being next to the other – here I think it is important how fragmentary they are – drifting in and out of each other – so hearing them – and small, how small they are – so hearing them one next to another – so speaking them – over and over – in varied relation they tug and push with sound and sense as lines might do to other lines – a kind of tuning – a kind of tumbling – the physical experience is simple – I write them – and then I type them up – and then I read them and white them out and read them and write things down and move around and type them up – and years pass –

light
in sky and breath
from thoughtful people
fills the air

I'm patted down
like wet green grass
the wind has blown my hair a bit

▪

passed cloudlet
now plunked down
and with
a folocule of looking
came that light
into my head

Think about understanding – the understanding impulse includes some desire to be done – some desire to complete the experience – that one might get on to new experiences – new poems – but there is something inherently indiscreet about a meaningful poem – it is in yourself or someone else or the world making meaning, and meaningful things are always in motion – by the very nature of us (people) finding them that way –

Fire on it
like a Dante
to his pigeon

one day
disposed
of oxygen
by flame

the poem in flux – the reader in flux – the magnetic relation of poems to each other – them shifting – tugging – pulling each other into alignment – and it's less mystical than it sounds – if I have a pile of small poems – go through it – read it – listen – and it is not the moment of any one thing – but a shared momentum tumbling together – the relational push and pull – you hear a sound – you hear a sound repeated – in feeling those things – sometimes recognized – your relation to both is changed – and theirs to each other – in being recognized but just in being, too – you are writing moving listening your way through – it's how the poems get made – as you bring new poems into their space – time – and each new relation with each new neighbor poem – causing shifts and changes – like a rock tumbler – sanding each other down – cracking and smashing – parts chipped off – then sanded down again – and the forming – so separate it seems at moments it can exist – which maybe is only that reading impulse – to return to the poem – not to be removed – not to be removed from the others and on its own – but that way of not being done that sends you back around by way of the beginning – or any other place for that matter – and all this being aloud & together provoking a kind of batted-around echo in the world – and it is locating – temporary and eventual –

pulsing walkish
grey on elevated train
up here all day grow weeds
as I'm sure you've seen
and bees

▪

crows landing
in trees and rust of

rusted scaffolding
by train I went
to sleep
and woke again

I'd shift – within a single page – lines and spaces – words and lines – everything staying or leaving the single page – those single pages being the space – each up next to the other – guides & neighbors – a moving back and forth was happening – a bouncing of tones and movements – changing or not changing – each poem would almost responsively solidify between its neighbors – and moved it might do it some more – until that solidifying became real – a responding – and that solidifying was for me – so that I was in a way then done with it – or done with it for then – and I could just blow through it – with my voice – the other kind of making, that is changing, put away –

sea
cloud
folds
up
under
curtain
then big
light in
on my
body
tapping

this reading aloud I think – I hear it – reading the poems over is certainly writing – a kind of writing – even not looking – not listening to them –

feels a kind of writing – there in its pile left with the others and its potential – it is easy to imagine putting poems away as a kind of dead stop – but what about letting them settle – settle into themselves – so they can be returned to clearly with just a bit of dusting off – or maybe as likely their mess takes over – they start to grow together or mold – a kind of compost that leaving alone making becomes – and us out in the world – changing – so different upon return as well –

and all this living happened – and as it did the poems started to acquire new formal ways about them – I would see it sometimes and sometimes I wouldn't – sometimes they would feel like the slight peculiarities of one poem repeated in another – sometimes more clearly they'd appear – and maybe the most obvious and peculiar was having the titles in the interior of the poems – most of my poems are untitled – and it made sense that this would happen – the poems not really wanting to start or finish the way titles seem to cause them to – I found I would just underline when met with the impulse to title – and so there where it happened it would stay – sometimes in the middle – anywhere – sometimes in the end –

caution still
    on cold flat boards
adellated and filling
    a brown pouch
        with food

<u>Melville's Companionship</u>

and more apples I'm gonna bring
to the revolution

calm latticed soul
of a thought rolled over
with a finger

I came down
to see myself
for a sort of conversation
and then

The Big North Pacific Ocean

& other things appeared in the middle of poems – as part of the poems – as much part of the poems as anything else – dates and places parenthetically – interior – or dedications – so that the person was right there where they were – where they are –

spectral and
dashing as leaves
in sunlight
are
they're turning
(for Cindy)
in front of things
quiet
quiet and
in
time

it sounds as I say it now so purposeful and willed – but really it was just about letting it all happen in the time it was happening – a kind of thing done aloud – and listening –

I like taking in
little bits of cloud
from paintings
and from towns
feet cold on ground
me still standing around

▪

this wise and wilting
thought upturned

a sweet wet cast
of the day did come
and my red bruise
which was a burn
pulsed like a lip
or like a tongue

listen and the oscillation of feeling and effect – as the balance of something coming into view – its recognition and surprise – there's no purchase on it – it is spans of time reanimated – vaporous particles of meaning constituting temporarily – you see the cloud you see it there you enjoy its form – you accept the unequivocal temporariness of it – and I want for a moment – you to think of the poem as a temporary accumulation of resonances – and the poem in time the way music is in time – basically there when it is happening – and the text is a score and the poem is that thing that happens when you animate it – beyond its thingness – the poem is an unassessable accumulation of those animations –

Mountains still there

and islands
winter's coming
in the sun
in the sun's light

these things agree
the falling leaves
from half-green trees
an open season rings
sound
unrestfully believed

then time's long day
is done in sleep

held together by that magnetic tension – of rhyme – creating loops in loops – and they were encouraging of each other – a line and a sound would echo – in a kind of dialogue – and from that resonance a poem would appear – and from that poem the reading and reading the hearing and hearing it – some triggering sound my body would respond to with reply – and the rhyme functioned somehow emotionally cyclical – patterned states done – wrapped-up it felt – too simply it seemed – circular – what were they saying – what were they making me say –

Patterns
clear & cutted up
I tried
good luck then
charging into
sky
my white cloud frowned:
What now?
I ended up here
don't ask me how

One of the pleasures – maybe one of the worrisome pleasures of rhyme is its ability to suspend – to allow an ungrounding of sense or meaning until one has comfortably arrived at the end of a line, the rhyme – so the experience of these was that they encouraged each other, that they multiplied, that the loops and turns grew dynamically extending – within the poem that suspension – and even at times with that extended release it became all that –

babes coo-cooing
and birds catching
skylight too
circle-faced boys
ensaucering whoms
the day acting true
they did something for me
and I did something for you
yup, that's the tune

hoo hoo
hoo hoo
hoo hoo
hoo hoo

So there was a time when they had to be put away – they had moved me – my body – into a responsive abstraction of sound – and everything that got started would instantly circle back on itself – so I couldn't read them anymore – I put them away – and started again – again and again this attempted present – and not just these rhymed ones – I found batches of poems everywhere – it seems all the time I'd just set them away – I had been – I didn't realize – doing it – now I see it – there just would have been too many – I wanted – I needed the cycles of them – batches circulating and responding – then shoved or tossed away – some floating sense of eventual return –

I'm not sure how to explain it – but putting them away – at times – felt more like sharing them – or maybe it was the me of then staying with them in some way – while the me of now moved on – and I like sharing them – sharing them privately – individually as offhand gifts to the world or people – I think the space of making the poems I was making made a space for making poems everywhere – some being in the presence of others differently – they were barely there as things – slight and gestural – that I could be – that I could be alive, too – in some way –

friends
dead air
fills empty
paths for walking
too
I came
to walk then
emptied out
no you
no you

I'd send them off in letters to friends – or keep them in that way that is for another person – but kept – waiting for James one day (and actually the same thing with Susie I remember) – waiting for them to come by – writing one – just to be waiting more presently – with them – excited to be with them – and not sharing it I guess to be more with them too –

crushed and ragged
piece of street
in which I waited
all morning
my tongue
and my face
feel no thing anymore

There's a time when I started thinking about the book – I wanted the social experience of sharing expanded – being in people's lives – over time – entering – returning to – being lived with – shared – made private – and in relation to you – being physical things – Bashō used to slip a poem into the conversation, and if it went unnoticed it was a success – I think of those and the unsuccessful ones, too – never even getting written down – just awkwardly remaining a part of the conversation – and some poems find the outward quality of a private experience fulfills in all ways their outward needs – or the poem you kept reading all summer – meaning all *that* summer and not this – or writing – imagine an occasional poem unwittingly making the occasion along with it – and they're lost as many private little gifts – like breath – still entering the air – ephemeral and real –

storm left flat
green leaves
still

and a little
bucket of
flesh-colored fruit

the poems themselves mimicking – a little batch away as I tucked myself away – the poems sent or shed – in relation to the needs – or social impulses –

caused and gaunt from
love with thoughtless persons
and day's flat heap of news
this life's a moon
and in some older time
was planets too
a trying voice
spoke be home soon

■

sleep a fitted
sleep I lay
there in my bed
a kind of dried out me
this high plain too
the cactus and the heat

but quickly they flower
their roots I read

In all the different places I went the search seemed to be for the most private – intimate – I was saying I didn't want to separate from the physical experience of writing them – of them coming to be – even in sharing

– handing over a small pile – standing nearby – my only copies – or just reading them aloud – to people – or with them – or them to me – that private thing made private again –

> This arching bit
> of tumult too,
> too smoothed.
>
> Like a man
> propped against
> a wet glass wall
> unpresent.

■

Twist of eye
and yes
                              I walked my dog
       in the cold park today
       beneath the sprouting trees
                colored finally mustard
         green, thinking
              capture maybe
            in yourself
             a few simple thoughtful things

and these two had floated around from the beginning – with others constellating – there are poems to which others are attracted – around which others grow – there are poems that lead and poems that gather – poems that propel and construct the ones around them – and so for me these were in a real way – they are – they remain – at some center of things – but none of these poems – none of the ones you heard today – are actually in the book – I wrote hundreds and hundreds of poems – also, I made that book – which is something else – and the lives of these poems are just different – not better – not worse – not something more or less successful – their lives just continue in a more private fashion – except for maybe moments like this, when they poke out their heads and say hello.

ACKNOWLEDGMENTS

The Bagley Wright Lecture Series on Poetry supports contemporary poets as they explore in-depth their own thinking on poetry and poetics, and give a series of lectures resulting from these investigations.

"The Lives of the Poems" was given at Gonzaga University, at New York University, and at the University of Arizona Poetry Center in Tucson. Thank you to Tod Marshall at Gonzaga University, April Heck at NYU, Tyler Meier at the University of Arizona Poetry Center and their respective staffs for welcoming the Bagley Wright Lecture Series into their programming, and for collaborating on scheduling, promoting, introducing, and recording these events. The Series would be impossible without such partners.

The author would like to thank Anthony McCann who was a close companion and regular responder to these poems over the years, and Jon Beacham (The Brother in Elysium) who published a number of the poems in various forms.

THREE TALKS

THE
BAGLEY
WRIGHT
LECTURE
SERIES

JOSHUA BECKMAN

THREE TALKS

WAVE BOOKS

SEATTLE AND NEW YORK

Published by Wave Books

www.wavepoetry.com

Wave Books titles are distributed to the trade by

Consortium Book Sales and Distribution

Phone: 800-283-3572 / SAN 631-760X

Library of Congress Cataloging-in-Publication Data

Names: Beckman, Joshua, 1971— author.

Title: The lives of the poems and three talks / Joshua Beckman.

Description: Seattle : Wave Books, [2018]

Identifiers: LCCN 2017001232 |

ISBN 9781940696423 (trade paperback)

Classification: LCC PS3552.E2839 A6 2017 | DDC 811/.54—dc23

LC record available at https://lccn.loc.gov/2017001232

Designed by Quemadura

Printed in the United States of America

9 8 7 6 5 4 3 2 1

First Edition

INTRODUCTION

When I was first asked to give these lectures, I imagined the results as some refined expression of the concerns that have propelled me as an artist. I expected that a responsibility to the request and to the form would likely result in a comprehensible articulation of what had been for much of my life allowed to be a messy cosmos of impulse and sense. I looked forward to finding out what I had learned or what I had come to know, and I looked forward to sharing that with others. As an artist there is a sense that what propels my endeavors are the growing and the shedding of these ways of knowing, but that they exist in an almost intangible form, forcing me constantly to echolocate, adjust, and be, but never really to know. And it is in this unknowing place where I have always found art.

But what I think I was being asked to do was to expose or to stabilize something inside my way of being an artist, and the idea (simply the idea of that) was very compelling. Compelling I think because I had always enjoyed seeing others do it. I had enjoyed the private letters, diaries, and writings of others on their own work. I had enjoyed lectures and essays in which artists tried to approach a narrative or philosophy of their own practice, and I had enjoyed artists critiquing others as a way of understanding themselves. But in all of what I appreciated, I realize now, was the basic failure and inability to enclose and explain. What I had appreciated was the sparks of disagreement or the expanse of tangential imaginative response they caused. And it was less the clarity than the attempt that I loved.

I am and have been for some time a fairly sick person, and it seems clear to me now how much a role that bodily circumstance played in how I came to write these talks. I began working on them in earnest in a hotel room about five years ago. Due to the collapse in my health, I had to leave the apartment I was living in, and I have found myself since that time in various homes, accommodations, and facilities, most often without my books. For me, my books (my library) seem to contain some expansive region of memory, one that feels at times the base or span of my self and imagination, the place where what I know resides. And at no point in the past five years have I really been able to access them. And much of that time was a sort of reimagining of my experiences with them, through the lens of a falling-apart self, so it should not be very surprising that these talks are more full of ramble and search than find.

But what I did find was a self always returning to the stabilizing and destabilizing ways of poetry. As person and as creature, occupying or accessing brief fullnesses of self or dissipating and partial in communal encounter. I found, as I have since I first experienced poetry, that the dead were at least as present and capable in life as those living around me, and that the friendships with them were as deep and constant, as challenging and various as my living relations (and their mutual influence had in fact made it impossible to believe the two categories distinct or for that matter even different). In one way or another all three of these talks are about those friendships, and all three come from a life of experiencing art as an aspect or expansion of the idea of friendship.

NOTE: First off I should say that the notes that make up the talk on anonymity and the poetic diary are just that. There is no recorded version of the actual talk, which went through various improvisational iterations, and which after the last seemed to be forming itself around an idea of social fluidity and bodily decay. Instead of trying to reconnect or finish it, I have left the notes as they were in an attempt not to get too far from the original endeavor. For the second talk, I read each example poem twice, only identifying it and its author between the recitations, so there was never a fully clear delineation between the poetry and prose, enacting (I think) in a little way some aspect of the porousness I was discussing. Finally, the talk on books was given at the Woodberry Poetry Room at Harvard University and from the library's collection we put together a corresponding small show including original works by Emily Dickinson and Henry David Thoreau, as well as the handwritten manuscript of *Friendship* by Ralph Waldo Emerson.

THE FRIEND, THE STRANGER & THE ANONYMOUS SPIRIT

NOTES FOR A LECTURE ON ANONYMITY AND THE POETIC DIARY

Everything in me can be summed up as an urge to be immediately something else; an impatience of the soul with itself.

FERNANDO PESSOA

I feel I am strange to all but the birds of America.

JOHN JAMES AUDUBON

When I was a teenager, I met this guy from New York City – his name was Phil and he was a photographer – a sort of thoughtful, classic street photographer – passionate and around twenty years old – we talked about his life and the city and he said that one of his favorite things to do was to go to Rockefeller Center – there are those two long walkways heading down to the best view of the ice rink – and he'd sit on the bench at the end of those walkways and wait – and before long and in constant succession – tourists would approach him and ask to have their pictures taken – or would, more accurately, begin the process of asking the question by making eye contact and showing their cameras – to which he would happily and repeatedly accept their cameras, take their pictures, and return their cameras – the photographs going off with them to be printed and kept – all day long – he is receiving the same question – human interaction of want and openness – and not exactly, *will you take our picture* – but something more like, *you? us?* – Phil was deaf, which you'd know if you heard him speak – but those spaces – different – spaces of relation and exchange – energy – public spaces alive with newfound proximity – shared currents of recognition – presence and anonymity – that knowing – always in movement – of being near – the sensual intimacy of public transportation – we bump into each other and we smell each other – a little droplet of spit on your arm – and that bodily being present – sensing and being sensed –

For me the endeavor of poems is greater than the poems – or the endeavor of poetry is poetry – not the writing separated from the finished object – not the finished object from the reading – the magic of the poems seems to me to be the amazing coexistence of all these states – social – collaborative and shared – before and during its making – constructed and formalized as its being read, etc. – I imagine it as an interpersonal state, like friendship – the poem sheds and regrows meaning as it is read – each time it's read – so that the reader sheds and grows selves – just to be present with it – echolocating our openness – and being there –

Out the window West and
    the set sun.
In the window a kerosene lamp
    whose light I write by.

experience moving and becoming – like plant cuttings – into verse record –

Out the West Window

Out the window West and
  the set sun.
In the window an oil lamp

one makes a cutting from a plant – you take that cutting – in some way it makes roots – it begins to grow – it's gathering nutrients from its soil – it's taking in the present sun – you make a cutting from that plant or two or three – all the plants still living – they're growing and changing too – all full plant made full – the same and other – all at once –

The sea tolls in the sky. Why
  at twilight do I
  have to write
all the world dropping off the West

That's late July 1959, John Wieners, day after day and then the next he writes:

Even my piss runs golden
in this time of plenty
all spring long one lovely
  flowering of my life, and
now in summer I come to
  this mountain, this morning
while below the mist rages. I range
  here clear in the secrets of
    my own being.

Let the peaks be blocked from view
the woman walks thru the room and
brother and sister sit together on the step
        of this stone house.

Lizard under the stone,
bees buzz around us
            in the morning
the two trees full of *canaries* and
            in the burnt grass
                        yellow poppies.

the air is alive with sound

Here – as I read it now – it bounces around between us – coming to be it seems – living – again each time – to be – the air is alive with sound – sounds of the written-down – now – in the morning – the two trees full of canaries – and in the burnt grass – yellow poppies –

In Japan the poetic diary has been for centuries a recognized form – and as in Japan the American poetic diary – allowing a flushing and fleshing out of the personal beyond distinction – of self or other – full mundane to ecstatic splat – it receives and allows as conveyance of human poetic impulse – expanding to include or narrowing to follow – malleable – because it's so personal – private – because it may stay so –

Branches bend
in the wind, leaves
wave thru the window at me,
        and whistle .

I'm very popular today.

Gloria, Carlos T., and Joan
are down at Steve and Nancy's

Male cat comes in thru the window
        to talk to me. The
room is filled with evening light
3 hours yet to sundown. Hey!
            it's summer!

(July 1971, Paul Blackburn)

▪ ▪ ▪

Bashō and Sora – three hundred years earlier – wandering off toward Kyoto – making poems with each other – beneath their rain hats walking around and encountering – being with others – the haiku they make and remember – the places they live and are in – that communal sense of a depository of shared theme – they add to – some poems made like dragging a magnet through one's living day to see what form the filings take – the magnetizing of self – and (and with) others – always some social sense of being in the poems made – the act of it temporary and uneventful (or really, maybe, temporary and mostly eventful) – not an understanding of being in the world – but inquisitive enactment of hows and whys –

Bashō found this – same time really as finding his name – "banana tree" – and its roots – part of his settling in – and then years later his champion, Shiki, changing to the cuckoo – in sickness – always repeating – seeing his life – ending – as one thing ending – death poems attempted and lived through – death poem attempted – the ending – from his sickness – worn bed-bound in 1899 – a verse record of peonies – living – there – this one small room –

In the alcove
The darkness of the peonies:
The wood thrush sings.

During the day my uncle visited me.

May 10th

. . . .

There is this silence
About the sickbed as the petals
Drop from the peonies!

Two flakes fall
And the shape of the peonies
Is wholly changed

Hyōtei came by in the morning. Saemon came in the afternoon and the painter Fusetsu in the evening. The paper cover of these sheets has become a picture with the falling blossoms.

Too weak to write – sick in bed – Saemon there to write it down for him – as passage from person to person – the so often anonymous conduit – of copy – pass and shed – as voice – the moving through – that moment in time – but also life – and I think of Shiki and Takuboku both dying young – their massive outpourings of work – Japan's last great attachment to haiku – the body – failing – sick – beginning the 20th century –

Takuboku writes:

> The desire to go where no human being exists has tempted me quite often of late. For a week, for ten days, for even a day, even half a day, it would be superb to lie down just by myself in a place where there are no people, where at least no human voices are audible, no, where at least I hear nothing which has any connection to me, where there is little fear that anyone will want to see me.
>
> In order to put these thoughts out of mind, I often go to a place crowded with people – the movies.

▪ ▪ ▪

The occupied spaces – lived shared spaces – experience and proximity – feeling individual and the challenge of that – I remember being on the subway once, with all the other people – and this little kid, getting off turned and said goodbye to us – as if we had all been there together – that livingness – a spell – and the space of it – as the dancer, articulating space, moves around – their bodies moving around in what seemed empty – and then are there – or there it is – or here we are – making spaces too – with poems – we make them – are in them – made by them – a resonance and accumulation – the poem more and more an experience –

I was in the park – it was basically empty and I could see these two kids performing this strange play – a kind of guerrilla theater in which one (they were about twelve or thirteen) acted like he was drunk and sleeping on a park bench – the other yelling and kicking at him – the entire time sort of doing it for me, who was walking by – and this moral play displayed clearly its convictions against intolerance or more violent disregard – and I sensed from their postures and how they moved as I walked away – I could hear a little of what they were saying – their disappointment in me for not intervening – I love the expectations they had of me – how callous the pleasure of seeing something could be – or seem –

▪ ▪ ▪

> Tonight I'm starting over – after these parenthetical months – for them – go real slow – like the first time going out after being locked up for ages –
>
> DANIELLE COLLOBERT

> Her simply seeking the anonymity of transience: to flee from the increasingly urgent desire or temptation to make extremes coincide.
>
> ANNE-MARIE ALBIACH

▪ ▪ ▪

The world's daze of living people – projected and made – how I saw the world come to be – before me – or as in it I arrive – imagine the world as the space for the first formation of the poem – not the page –

what can seem a controlled accumulation of refinements – really an act of finding – laying itself out – the strange and the near exchanging themselves in happening – and that echoing back – making its form –

The physical bodily presence of being in the world – as it is in the poem – or can be – the encounters with the dead – the dead and the living – the to be dead – the have been alive – the living in spoken voice of poem – the being with it – the being with the people there – the temporal joining of creatures in reading and being read – their shared being next to one another known or not –

Melville was in Rome, after touring the Vatican – and looking at the statues around the city – he went to the Colosseum and found it strangely overgrown and empty – he couldn't recognize it for what it had been or even what it was – until he populated it with the statued animals, warriors, and citizens he had seen earlier –

▪ ▪ ▪

> What I have written I knew little of until I had written it, *says Robert Creeley*. If at times I have said that I enjoy what I write, I mean that writing is for me the most viable and open condition of possibility in the world. Things have happened there, as they have happened nowhere else. . . . In poems I have both discovered and born testament to my life in ways no other possibility has given me. Can I *like* all that I may prove to be, or does it matter? Am I merely living for my own approval? In writing it has seemed to me that such small senses of existence were altogether gone, and that, at last, the world "came true." Far from being its limit or director, the wonder is that I have found myself to be there also.

▪ ▪ ▪

Kleist writes: "A man in the act of speaking finds a strange source of inspiration in the face of his listener; and a look that signals the comprehension of a half-expressed thought will often inspire us with the entire second half of the thought" – and it's not the comprehension really, but the face – the person there – the being together – an idea of audience – for me, the audience necessary for making a poem is a single person I may or may not recognize – who may or may not exist – I could mean my friend C_________, or you, or some not yet born or dead person – and the magic of the poem is that it will come to create that person – and the person's magic making a poem of that experience – someone else actually physically there doesn't always happen – sometimes you are just alone – no like souls around you – to continue on being alive would one have to believe in an unavailable but hugely generous individual listener – not to identify them or flesh them out or hope for their arrival but just with some abstract faith accept that their existence and the existence of the poem are joined – some current of belief – as in the stranger, that ecstatic possibility of friendship to be ignited – regardless of the profound infrequency with which that happens –

In that same essay Kleist writes, "One often sees, in a social gathering, when animated conversation produces continued cross-pollination of ideas, how some people, who usually remain silent because they do not feel that they are themselves very articulate, will suddenly, with a convulsive movement, flare up, grasp at suitable language, and thereby bring something completely unintelligible into the world" – and this is also how a poem might come to be.

▪ ▪ ▪

> Every day things happen in the world that can't be explained by any law of things we know. Every day they're mentioned and forgotten, and the same mystery that brought them takes them away, transforming their secret into oblivion.
>
> PESSOA

All this private language of familiarity – hearing it one becomes that other person or friend – the shared language – for that moment – an accepted openness met – where we join in encounter – enlivening and making real –

GONE NOW

David stepped into the falling snow falling in the parking lot.
cells – whatever guaranteed those billowing sails
in your head,
It's gone now

SUSIE TIMMONS

The poem embraced – it can expand – an opening that by its nature extends beyond the initial relation to how it was made – sometimes it happens while you are there – or later – echoes heard resonating – and partial – in your life – the indiscretion of it – and how the openness, its actualities are the real present thing – we see capability as strength – but it's weakness, too – being on the beach all day and then closing your eyes tight and then seeing that beach again – a private blood pulse of feeling and presence – or lack – like acts of passive corruption – bodily demand and seizure – each tiny physical effect – my ears to bells – a kind of cone-like ringing – through which in the park I hear wheels and voices –

■ ■ ■

3 WEEKS NOW. Since Tues 27 May and she still doesn't know. Still hasn't been told . . . She goes on planning planting looking forward. Though wondering what is wrong. Though not wondering so much aloud to me anymore. Guessing? Suspecting? Knowing it deep down perhaps? Not able to stay awake at night at all now. Nodding off in her chair by 7 o'clock though still insisting she going out to work tomorrow & I bound to the doctor's silence & can't say anything as I watch her . . . can't give no 'good reason' to stop her/ tell her why she shouldn't . . . And she feels already frail. And looks smaller And her features have somehow changed, I think . . . All the strength & power draining away . . .

Kamau Brathwaite – writing – *The Zea Mexican Diary* – days around the end of his wife's life – their selves tumbling and shedding – in some being – in some trying – to understand – the present – as it's always found – passing –

Only tonight Sunday 14 December

going through my haphazard Diary again did I come

across these entries - fragments - can't even tell you

how/when I wrote them - inserted here in square

brackets - written miraculously on her birthday - on

the day she died

■

▪ ▪ ▪

"I am writing to you today, urged on by a sentimental need – a sharp painful desire to talk to you. As can be seen very easily," writes Pessoa, it can be seen very easily by the fact that "I have nothing to say to you" – those are my favorite letters – their authors present before their mouths open – the idea of the letter and the intimate addressed space of the letter – how one has the expected attention of the listener – the recipient will read the letter when they are capable and attentive – or at least rushed on by an enthusiasm that is its own special way of attention – the sense that it was written for me – for me exclusively – or more really, to me wholly – for me wholly – that's why I feel you there in your letters – and so a responsive depth and richness follows – from that presence – each correspondence to some degree creates its language – the familiar and assumed clear as they are in conversation – a fluidity and private style –

i try to get on
w/ people

they owe me
i don't or

it's the wrong size
& i oversleep

put me back
two days   look

& i'll catch you
saturday

great

STEPHEN JONAS

filled with a voice and human presence – it exceeds tone – that they were written – that they make place – I live inside and there we are – together – I'm talking – I'm listening – we're all doing this together privately –

■ ■ ■

> The next thing that happened was that I was a very little older and we were in Vienna, a nice place then. And now there was something I could remember as well as some things I could be helped to remember by hearing them told again and again, then and later.

Gertrude Stein – saying things over – in function – like the personal repetition of private anecdotal histories – or hearing them that way –

> I like a thing they say if they say it every time they feel it. They say it of my dog Basket, every time they see him and they see him any time and they always say look at him you would take him for a sheep. And so all this time everybody in talking speaks of the Germans, they always were saying, but they are still strong, they are still powerful, just as Saint Odile said they would say and they have been saying it any day and every day and in every way whenever the Germans were mentioned by them and naturally with the war going on and the Germans being in occupation they were mentioned every day and any day and they always said well until a month ago, they always said with meditation or conviction depending upon the person speaking they said they are still powerful, they are still strong. To-day and every day they go on mentioning the Germans, and now any one of them and every one of them as they speak of them they say in the same way, they are pretty sick, and nobody says anything when the Germans are mentioned except that the Germans are pretty sick now, quite sick now, and that is what I like that they repeat every day what they feel each day and that is not repetition that is saying each day what they are knowing, that Basket the poodle you would think he was a sheep, that the Germans until September 1943 were still very strong, that the Germans in September 1943 are sick, pretty sick, quite sick.

■ ■ ■

José Rodrigues Miguéis – baffled by the fact of his brain tumor after years of hypochondria – *A Man Smiles at Death with Half a Face* – arriving at the doctors – writerly – an overwhelming complex of notes and attentions – about his self – his experiences – so much – basically incomprehensible –

The idea of making as it appears in the body – mine and others' – meds masking – the corrosiveness of decay – continue uninhibited – or the dissociations caused by knowing that some thing happened and is not happening – that you were not doing something and are not doing it – or forgetfulness –

Monks making private quiet homes – "They are the anonymous well-wishers who reduce the moral overdraft of mankind" –

The aphoristic voices of Antonio Porchia making their way into the prisons – shared – as if unauthored and anonymous –

Thomas Gray spending the last decade of his life mostly writing in the margins of Linnaeus's *Natural System* – a vast accumulation of plants and animals seen and noted – rarely leaving his home – but expanding out into the natural world –

Or Linnaeus himself at the end of his life – having lost much of his sense and memory – sitting around reading his own book not knowing who had written it, but enjoying it thoroughly –

I can't even tell what draws me to this – the un-bodied or the re-bodied – how that feels – or just privacy – exposure and privacy – "Today, I dragged my feet and my immense fatigue through the streets" – to take everything in with the consciousness of the senses –

"Weakness [is] the very Hallmark of Genius. [It provides] a point of least resistance in human nature, an opening through which the force of Nature might enter the human world" – Also the pain sometimes compounds and centralizes in a place in your body – later spreading back out – later gone –

sundaysundaysundaysundaysunday
sun
day
a quiet along the empty walks
single bird speaks to blue sky to
elm heavywith summer
EMPTY AND ALIVE
EMPTY AND ALIVE
EMPTY AND ALIVE
                The simple act of drinking a cup of coffee
                The simple act of pulling up one's trousers
buckling the belt . having shit, washed hands and face,
go to work . empty and alive . heavy with summer . light
with the promise of death . bright books in the bookcase,
window open, the day comes in, o fade the carcinoma, lay
down the two dollars, all those others rolling dice, but
it's my body, I'll bet on that . o, it floats thru the blood
with the greatest of ease . the pain goes and comes again . the

cat hunts in the grass, the gull swings over the sea, the blood
sings a very old tune . Take it
easy, it's sunday, no?
All day.

(that's Paul Blackburn, from his journal four months before he died)

5:20 & you can bet
it's A.M.   everybody
needs go work   . 2
cats cross the street
I need not
go work   .   I need
          – What are those 2 cats
                    doin'?

Meeting up with the poem in a place of – not accord – but necessary relation – a sense of the fullness of you and it – and by extension, its poet – recognized in the other – as when you speak uninhibitedly to a friend or lover or are heard – you hear – the hearing, fully – active and buoyant – as the speaking – and so that relation to what's been joined –

Autobiographer Biófilo Panclasta – Bió-filo meaning Life-Lover and Pan-clasta meaning All-Destroyer – writing little biographies of those he knew –

"Hope is a delicate suffering. Its waste products vary, but most of them are meaningful." LeRoi Jones – LeRoi Jones later Amiri Baraka and now both again –

The scribes of the Warsaw ghetto – writing in Yiddish – for which you could be killed – taking on some documentary task for the rest of your life – what you had seen – the others giving you their food – and then burying that writing in milk jugs before you died – translated and in a new world here –

Or John Clare – reading to his parents – his poems – them saying if only he could write like that – thinking they were copies made in practice – him hiding the truth – and stuffing them as insulation into the wall – his mother using them to light the stove – him not saying anything – to break the spell of their appreciation and watching them burn for fear of what knowing might bring.

FRIENDSHIP, POROUSNESS & THE INTIMATE EXPERIENCE OF POETRY

I was on Cape Cod – I saw a boy on the beach – he had a fishing pole – he was sort of walking around – and he had a kite attached to the fishing pole – I guess so he could hold it up – and so he could reel it in and let it out – and he looked like a little English boy with his shorts – and even now I just sort of picture him like two old etchings drawn together – the kite flying above him out of the picture – I walked around reading Cape Cod – that being alone – and in actual space – that actual space and sand and water – all those bodies washed up on the beach in 1849 – coldness – vastness and presence – kicking sand around and looking out at the clouds – the sense of form that finds itself constantly rearticulating in them – flying a kite you provide a tension – attempts at something physical – familiarity and awareness – you're pulling at it – it, in the air – air sometimes forms itself as wind – into winds – winds varying and indiscrete – so catching – causes form – a tension – gives it form –

What stories
bear repeating   news
of the day we demonstrate
the motions of earth   its shape

birds pass through trees, or sit
  watching or in song
    not sounding afraid
  eyes make walls

    dissolving stone but
          blinded
      the waves, seas, how forgotten
          stars dashed in the water

(that's Larry Eigner fifty years ago this week)

in world a kind of span – in span a kind of time – a presence – and a feeling cooperative – simultaneous – form realized and released – a temporary state and selfness – a meditation – a shared state – and a dispersal in that sharing – partly just because you're watching the kite move around in the sky while you're doing it with your hands – it's a physical thing like listening – or walking – that responsive presence propelled – or just a loafing and wandering about in it – but in it – a not getting there – getting there – or going – a kind of physical distraction – guided by attractions, concerns, and leanings – like walking – the poems free-form and moving – access and reflective space for the constant art of natural formation – like if a waterfall were made of the earth and rock it flows over – or just say clouds – the forming and changing of themselves – making themselves –

Even while they are existing in a book, all those words are out there doing other things – while you're reading them in your poem, they are out there in the world as well, kinda polyamorous, suggestible and infinitely occupied – and I feel as though I am trying to recognize it as something temporary – through the experience of writing – in the same way it appears temporary through the experience of reading – capable of remaining – temporary – moments of today – the way it elevates out –

the heat obliterates
 the walls of the house
  indoors. outdoors. the children's
   cries
    the birds keep on
   and cars go by

(that's Larry Eigner again, the same time)

Sometimes I think of the poem as something discretely placed in time, that the appreciable experience of the poem happens primarily in the moment of engagement or reflection – but doesn't it happen so many other times too – and maybe that's not even it – maybe it's just that things that are alive or were alive don't seem finite – when dead seem gone, sure – but seemed gone at other times too – and seem here sometimes, alive – even now – and poetry falls into that space between – when reading aloud, confronted by embraced real presence – you are there – in the poem – among the enacted world – which happens when poems are getting made as well –

I think of the haiku poets traveling and making poems – spirit of openness – haiku as conduit, response, and proof – so the life of the haiku poet is to exist and integrate thoroughly and fluidly into that existence the poetic act – the ways of being in the world are in its way – through its way – a kind of metabolism – social – shared – and this feels strange if you are considering a poem as a singular thing – some unalterable bit of perfection – finite and resolute in its completeness – and that's just one way to think about poems – but isn't it more organic and changing –

Centuries and centuries of spoken poems – of stories constructing and happening – the encounters of people – in space and time they are made to exist – if people are there you speak to them – change for them – that story as you speak to them – various repetitions and highlit senses become central – a kind of guidance – think of the troubadours coming to town wandering around and incorporating the people they found into their tales – drawing them toward the spots where they would eventually perform – an audience now an active visible part of the narrative – following to hear what happens to them –

And it's not just the oral traditions – think of ancient fragments anecdotally kept and written down – think of samizdat editions and desperately scribbled copies – think of the entire practice of translation – think of Walt Whitman changing his one book and many poems over and over again – or Emily Dickinson leaving countless private variants to be considered – all the variorum editions of our most esteemed poets – and most poems never end up in print at all – private accumulation of drafts to be gone through or not – but still to exist – variant and real – and now in the 21st century it's basically moot again –

Easy to Love
the POETS
Their
SPLENDOUR

Falling all over the pages
Extorting atomic rainbows

Easy to Love
the Poets

Their

SPLENDOUR
Falling all over the pages
into
My lap

(that's Elise Cowen)

I'm trying to imagine now the central experience of the poem as something temporary – and so I imagine it as something aloud – something spoken out – or aloud inside you – a muscular compulsion – the livingness – a spell – and the space of it – as the dancer articulating space, moves around – their bodies moving around in what seemed empty – and then are there – or there it is – or here we are – making spaces too – with poems – we make them – are in them – made by them – a resonance and accumulation – the poem more and more an experience – a flash of being –

When I step through the door
everything has changed. Finally,
it is out the door
past homes, down the trail
the lovely beach
draws me into her drawing. Finally

I am past the fear of life's paucity.
 Green Angels, stream, in hot California
and in the stillness seeds popping.

(Joanne Kyger)

A reading and writing kind of closer to drawing than painting – drawing, its incomplete presence allowing in – its fragmentary way essential – it's what it is – time – traditional painters using drawing as a way to identify borders – by going through them over them – by failing in ways their paintings couldn't – in ways they didn't want their masterpieces to fail –

I think of Emerson – his saying that friendship is the masterpiece of nature – or really, he says it "may well be reckoned the masterpiece of nature" – that this conception of masterpiece is unfixed – that it is moving – that it will remain so – always in flux – temporary – I'm thinking of clouds again and people – but also that it can only be understood – that it can only be recognized fully from the inside – privately – intimately – so the masters concerned with their masterpieces would make these drawings – these studies – seeing the edges – of the visible – and to do so ceding all sorts of control – and accuracy – to something expressive and spontaneous – how else find the look on that person's face or the emotion in that stone house – and there is something about this drawing – this unrestrained extension beyond – embraced in the poem – the improvisation, sure, toward art – but also, as art – the act as art, as poetry – the partial – the social – the bodily – the private – the free –

I feel friendship's continual presence – the way a poem might stay with you – a poet – the exuberant passions – and attractions – the being consumed and inside of it – everything in and through it – I feel the poem unrestrained – sincerely present – and improvisational – at its core an exposure of unknowing – complex and unanswered – unconcerned with propriety or etiquette – the freedom that is friendship – the consent to accept – that allows the friend, unrestrained, to speak – and to be heard – not immediately designated or judged – but encountered – I think it's that I found in the poems when I found the poems I loved – some ecstatic circuit's been joined – and that's how friendship feels –

I remember a terrible professor in school saying that if you put a Rembrandt on a cliff and pushed someone off the cliff – its expression wouldn't change – anyhow, that's one argument – and of course there are plenty of arguments for that but I wonder – what I wonder is why accept or demand that set of values if what you want is something more communal – if your presence is already demanding another communal place – we isolate and individualize – but it is just a ridiculous notion – to propose a separation of one human from the other ones –

I found you
came in the room and started talking,
and ironing
I turned on the radio, the night rose
around us
I forget,
you
were looking at me. I came in the room

and started ironing. The night rose
around us. The pinnacles, the far off
spines of trees like
the lakes
under us, hollow
stones to go through, in the distance, close, the eye
brings the breeze under us,
through us, over us

(Joanne Kyger)

I'm moving with the poem – I've found it – I can hear it – the experience of reading and listening – aloud – it's something so surprising – more future than past – you can recognize it – and you can tend to it in a way – the other things disappear – and you move through the space of the poem – in the poem's present – some other present receding – I'm hearing and speaking at the same time – my lips moving when I write – and this is what I'm feeling about reading aloud – reading aloud I get drawn to stand up – I expand my chest – I move my arms – I rock or sway – my head or jaw bobs in some strange rhythmic fashion – or I whisper or I mumble – I close in my shoulders – my body making intimate my reverberations – just moving my lips to make and hear – the words form – physical and sounding out – over and over touching my lips to each other – and if I cover my mouth, there my breath is on my hand – or close my eyes and hear a line –

I become occupied by the poem – breathing as it breathes – or talking as it talks – some poems call on you to act as they act – perform their performance – I find myself in some dramatic pose when I read Frank O'Hara – "Khrushchev is coming on the right day" – the experience a sort of cinematic pleasure – like one might find in front of the mirror – or in the shower –

"My dear reader, read aloud, if possible!" writes a 19th-century philosopher. "If you do so, allow me to thank you for it; if you not only do it yourself, if you also influence others to do it, allow me to thank each one of them, and you again and again! By reading aloud you will gain the strongest impression that you have only yourself to consider."

There are some poems that attempt to release and exhale – exaggerations of affect – and some of those exhalations become poems – and some of the freer breathings become poems – and in reading them the body comes to be differently – not acting out at all – just being –

WAITING

over the lilacs won't he   come home

to at least rest tonight,   I want to see

the round car safe in the driveway, cinders

and the moon over head

(Joanne Kyger)

I feel different, and it all feels like a counterbalance to the annoyingly persistent sense of self that seems so intent on being itself – and allows at times a sense of self that feels outside of my self – but still there – right in my self as well.

▪ ▪ ▪

There's this therapeutic practice in which the therapist touches the patient or asks the patient to do some physical task like holding on to the table edge or their own hand – and in doing this – occupies the body of the patient – and directs the conscious mind of the patient to that occupation – and reading aloud can be basically the same thing – a guide provided – so you are occupied in the bodily performance of it – your conscious critical mind applied to the task – the self of you in a cloud of experience – sound and sense – and the performing of it – the body pulsing – with its own enactment – the reverberations in one expressive and real – the space and zone engaged – as one might in the world world – unattributing and human – like wandering around –

Then the poem experience causing experience in everything – its effective potential on myself – of that – of what to me is recognizable – or some way bodily – sensually attended – spiritually present – a compostable mass always heaving and sprouting – sores and flowers on the pile – things microscopic – the glass fashioned full – the brutal physicality of actions and their results – after their results – or is the poem a reflection of a combination of physical needs – I need my voice my body my spirit to make these sounds and so out they come – out to meet those needs – the result of writing those poems being that those things got said – and the experience of reading being I said them –

I saw myself
a ring of bone
in the clear stream
of all of it

and vowed,
always to be open to it
that all of it
might flow through

and then heard
"ring of bone" where
ring is what a

bell does

(Lew Welch)

A friend calls up and says "monks reading rules as devotional forms" – I play it over a bunch of times – monks' monkhood being the ways read aloud – I remember hearing the answering machine – the way you'd be at attention – that moment – you'd be there in that presence of being talked to – no, spoken with – some strange thing that was made and barely existed – until it got heard – some faithful expanse of time between leaving it and then – like a letter – and then it being listened to – and then it being gone –

The loose attachment to forms and things as they pass – that even whole you move by – the sense of being – there – increases – forms of attended things temporarily present – washes of sense and place – as with consciousness – that one at times recognizes one's own form – states – it inhabits – you inhabit it – spans of distance and the energy they release – the disinhibiting of expressive responsive presence – making poems – making poems sound out – in ways – in new ways – those private newnesses I feel when the poem comes out of me aloud – my self and world more open – each time you read – experience sheds knowing – it acquires new knowings – each time a kind of regeneration and simultaneous decay – the poem feels alive –

the discursive how
packed
lives

and by the echo

dissolved

as the
forcing together

a pile of screens
you could leave acquire
time,   flies
reverberating

the dark house, and the vast
sun moving, out,
slowness, level of it all

approach night

the clouds to the sea

stirred   on

(Eigner again, from November 1959)

The inside space as one feels with sound – one's body vibrates with a sense of things – and so a continuous climate of sensation – even expression – as one feels when one listens to music and is alive with that music – a kind of expressive attention – a part of what is happening – one feels essential – not the distance of appreciation or even some collaborative necessity to the completion of the work, but vibrating and responding so that characteristics of you and it become shared – in a way as music is often consuming – listening you can become part of it – the blood in your body, your skin too – sometimes your muscles and bones and everything – sometimes you dance around – sometimes your pulse calms, etc. –

And I wonder to what extent this is allowed by the general expectation that music's receiver is not the intellect – rarely does one apply that type of intelligence to a listening experience – imagine the fluid role of thoughts actions emotions one finds in listening and how easy on one's self one is in that dumb overtaken state – or the theoretical drifting one does while listening – that one's mind wanders – that one is unsettled – that the sensual experience seems to dominate does not make us feel any less that we are aware of what we have heard – in fact we can feel the proximity of the meaning (no, of a meaning) of the art despite our inability to define it – in fact it may be that like certain human instances and relationships, we are capable of the meaning only as we remain unable to complete it with definition – to understand is to complete – to try to understand is to try and complete – and for a poem, which is a real thing, a living thing – organic and changing – capable sure, of a different kind of life than, say, a botanist or a flower – but still so capable of interactive presence as to deny its inanimate status –

So to desire to understand fully – (fully, being the more important word) – is the desire to complete, and the completion of the poem is the death of the poem – and here it feels important to state that the desire for some, or much, understanding – the prodding and pointing at parts of the poem – the isolation of the language so that its use may be comprehended – the parsing of part from part – the assessing of sound or any particular of the poem – the investigation of underlying philosophies histories biographies etc., decoding deciphering to name a few – none of these are of course in and of themselves detrimental – simply, I'm proposing that if one leads with the intellect one can find oneself done with the poem (some way or another, soon enough), and that that being done can be a kind of betrayal of the poem. If you don't care for the poem or the poet, that betrayal is not such a concern – but if you don't care that much for the poem I suggest you stop reading it and allow its fragmentary self to be – to move on –

THE LANGUAGE

Locate *I*
love you some-
where in

teeth and
eyes, bite
it but

take care not
to hurt, you
want so

much so
little. Words
say everything.

I
love you
again,

then what
is emptiness
for. To

fill, fill.
I heard words
and words full

of holes
aching. Speech
is a mouth.

(Robert Creeley)

That experience of knowing bodily – of self being in some place – being present in that place – not just the conjuring of places and things that are and make the environment of our poems – that moment and its castings are the poem – not that you understand them but that they are there –

I think of the most impassioned communications – as crying fights blown out with fragmented abstractions of hurt and anger – mostly partial and repeated words and sentences – interrupting and unfinishing itself so one might be – inside a swim of words and sound – without comprehensively expressed thought – but meaning more full – and the other more pleasant passions act the same too – abstraction can be porous like that – that folding cavalcade of words – words with their images their thought and resonance – meant to allow an attentive drift almost meditatively forming – meaning temporarily held –

I like reading like that – I think feeling like that's when the poem's a live rush or faucet-like pouring out – you'll go through it and just have to go through it again – the forming – the coming together – I was reading – in the center – this idea about porousness – the core of art – its making – its appreciation – and time the distraction that is access –

AN IRREGULAR ODE

Once I began to write,
Be ruled by Beauty & her wilfullness
& got no further
Choking and wheezing, subject completely to the selfishness
of my own history

I don't wonder that you doubt my love
My attention wanders even now, squinting at the moon
bamboo blinds – I should be with you
we're only blocks apart

The same imaginary beauty splits us up, I keep chasing
the one who invents the mountains and the stars
I'm a fool supposing she's someone else than you
are moss & ferns in forest light

(Philip Whalen)

ON BOOKS

So, I had this idea to talk about a walk, or really to try and take you all on a walk. I feel at times the kind of attention one is open to on a walk is not dissimilar to the kind of attention that can guide one through a poem. By a walk, I mean something between a stroll and a hike, that movement into the outside world with a hope of encountering it. The kind of walk, which if someone asked what you were doing you would say *I'm going for a walk*. That kind of walk. You feel things you notice things, your body is activated and engaged. It is constantly making intuitive and sensual decisions. You see something and look at it, or you see something and move around it. You hear and smell and touch. Sometimes you wander off with your mind and you are very much far away from the actual physical world you are moving through. Sometimes you are taken by something – a scrap of paper on the ground or an animal or anything and it draws you toward, it draws your attention toward. And then mostly on you continue with your walk, parts of it elevating in meaningfulness and parts of it floating away almost completely unnoticed.

I think about reading a poem. When I read a poem – I say it aloud – even when I'm reading it to myself – I move through it. The saying it aloud, which is hearing and speaking at the same time, feels to me like the guided and unguided aspects of a walk. And in many ways, poems are the temporary things that occupy the spans of time it takes to see them or hear them or read them. The walk with the endless mystery of its uncontrolled and unfolding perspective can feel like the poem – while we easily recognize their stable characteristics, we can feel, especially in the acts of deeply encountering them, some aspects of the accumulated moments of poems experienced – those moments inside the actual words on the page without you, and now made alive as depth-full presence. Reading the poem aloud – mostly just keeping going and taking things in as it is read. One knows one is missing something and one knows one is accessing something as well. My idea with the poem is that it is to be experienced.

Often when I'm reading I will gather the books around (sometimes on the kitchen table or other tables in the house) and keep them together so that even just moving by them excites some idea or memory. Little connections knocked against you during your day. One is reminded (almost sensually) of the things those books are when walking back and forth by them.

It's like a memory – holding the peripheral meanings that swirl around it, elevated by the structure of its central concerns identified or not. And I was reading Stevenson and I was reading Thoreau, too. So there were all the Thoreau books and Stevenson books on my kitchen table and I read this in Stevenson, "The woods by night, in all their uncanny effect, are not rightly to be understood until you can compare them with the woods by day." And when I read it, I instantly remembered Thoreau having said (earlier that week) in his journals, the journals in which he is often documenting his night walks through Concord, that one does not know the day until they have walked at night. And then I remembered Stevenson, saying of Thoreau that he was dull and priggish and unfriendly. And not having ever met him, one gets the distinct impression that he is just fine not having ever met him. And so here they are together on my table saying, not surprisingly, seemingly opposite things. One, that you don't know the day until you walk at night, and the other, that you don't know the night until you walk at day. And I kept thinking that now, at least for me, those things were basically the same thing. Years after they are gone, years after there is nothing they can really do about it, I have put them together and think fondly of how similar they are. Look, I thought, they both enjoy walking at night.

Thoreau, constantly writing journals of his daily experience, taking and forming from those journals his books – almost like cuttings from a plant to be given away, to go grow in other people's homes. And Stevenson, who made formed things from the imagination to go activate the imaginations of others, so giving and playful. Both struggling with ideas of place and home (one traveling constantly, the other notably still) and both dying at forty-four, leaving behind the uninhibited refuse of their committed literary lives. I would think of the writers, their selves present in their books, their similarities and differences, just right out there for me to sort of endlessly engage in. One basic thought of the book is as a continued them, and their lives reanimated in their public and their private selves presented so vigorously in print, and sort of multiplying in the attentions to them. And while this idea felt like it could be a real response to time and the solidity of the object, it felt so strange pairing the two of them up and making them do that. As if just because there on my table they were, they had to talk.

There are these fantastic stories from the 18th century about the lives and communications of books. There are poems really about every part of a book animated and talking to every other part. The covers to each other, the bookplate complaining to its contents about where it has ended up, or the poem itself calling to be set free from the confines of the boards holding the pages in. Or the other conversations of books with each other. Like Swift's *Battle of the Books* – them interacting on the shelves and speaking with each other, introducing each other, berating each other. Ancient and modern tomes bickering over the respect or lack of respect one is given or deserves. The moral of the story of all the books beginning to speak to one another is usually that in no case will it result in them getting along. And this is blamed naturally on the character of the reader, on the reader's inherent disregard for the differences in the books acquired – to have so many different efforts brought together – to encourage so many unlikely relationships – or at least encounters – and the ability to unbalance seems at the center of the experience of life with books – the visions and ways each conjure – their different tones and languages – their voices and the places they bring us, the places they want to go.

And so I thought that if I was going to talk about books, maybe I should just take you on a walk, but on a walk through a library and have each book sort of do the explaining for itself. And then I started thinking about which library, thinking about the different types of libraries and how books come together in them. Not just what happens when they do, but how they end up where they are. It's hard to talk about one library without wanting to talk about all of them. And which one would I choose? And then I thought not to take that walk but just to list and present all the different kinds of libraries – the public ones gathered and arranged systematically by many people over years and years, the private ones in individual homes constructed intuitively over a single lifetime. And others like the temporary ones you take away on a trip, the books one might throw in a bag for a walk, or the trunk of a car – I think of Joshua Slocum sailing alone around the world in the 1890s, rigging up his boat to keep moving and it sailing on while he went below deck to his little library and read *Moby-Dick*. Or the imaginative libraries, like the one that grows over time between two friends (made up of the books they actually share but also the ones they talk and think about, too, the ones they associate with each other). Or the private library inside of the public one, the books you go back to over and over again and take out and how they become yours. It's so rare that a book is out there on its own, removed from the others.

Thomas Gray notoriously wrote in books that belonged to anyone – if he saw a mistake or something he thought could use clarifying or expounding upon – and it seems his university library (and libraries as far afield as right here) are still full of books that are full of his scribbled notes. And I thought I could just write about him – poet, private scholar, marginaliast, friend – correspondent, whose private communications inspired countless public ones, whose descriptive letters of the Lake District are as responsible as any other work for the appreciation and enthusiasm of the Romantics for the place. The life of the book that is as much about the active experience of being inside them as writing them oneself. Gray writing so few poems, and considered to have stopped his literary output altogether the decade before his death, but the reality was that he was writing in the margins of his books, most notably his copy of Linnaeus's *Natural System* (a catalogue of living things) – writing on every bare spot of it, writing and drawing pictures – hundreds of notes in English and Latin, that spanned the mundane to the poetic – practical and imaginative, at one moment describing the inspiring forceful movements of the wings of a bird in flight and the next describing how tasty or salty it was.

And now I was just getting desperate. I had tried so many things. I went back and read the description of the lecture I was to give. There wasn't a walk anywhere to be found. I said I would talk about the intimate and communal experiences of poetry and how they relate to the book as an object, as well as the private library and the porous experience of the book in real and imagined space. Oh no. Was I really going to try and do that. What did it mean? I knew what it meant, but would I just go and enact it or would I take it apart and explain. For me the porous experience of the book was simple, it was the only way I had come to understand them. I would be eating a sandwich or I would be sweating and the oils in my skin would get onto the page or I would go to grab a book I hadn't gone to in a while and the dust would come off it, straight into my lungs. Or I would be walking down the street and the experience of some poem I had read earlier would reemerge in my walking self or maybe even in my words. I would say something and the voice of someone else or, even stranger, the impulse of someone else would come out of me, mixed with what felt like my own. And my experience of the real actual book, my experience of touching and holding it and having the poem close to me and my experience of the lives of the poems and poets that accompany me when I'm away from their books, blends completely with my self as a person, a reader, a poet. The porousness I meant is that things move in and out of you fluidly and not exactly effortlessly, but not in a controlled way either. It's an openness. That's what a pore is. And to think of what the poems I was reading were doing and how they were entering me and how aspects of them would come out of me at times. It is easy to think of it as feelings and understandings – you read a poem and its understandings of things enter you as understandings. Or feelings. You feel that in the experience of reading a poem and now that feeling is in you and capable of being had, and out into the world as feelings are sometimes sent outward. But really the porousness was about all the slight things, the ways and aspects of the poems that enter you unnoticed, or at least unidentified. And that's the closeness to the poem, I think. I had the idea that spending all of this time trying to figure out a way to make a lecture about something like books in the poet's life was just too much and had made me scattered and oblivious to the basic experience of standing up in front of a group of people and telling them about something. I couldn't, after all, stand up and tell you everything I've been thinking, and yet being with books sort of encouraged just that.

In Ruskin's *Elements of Drawing*, he berates the indulgent parent who gives the child too many books, so that instead of being forced to find the meaning within, the child can sort of browse and gather to their imagination's content. And that a few books, regardless of how good they are, are a better inspiration to the youngster. All I can really say is that it is probably sensible to heed this warning, but I have not, so sort and browse I continue to do.

I had been reading for years and I had been making notes for this lecture for years. I had a pile of paper scraps, and every time I would have an idea or a line would come to me I would scribble it down. And every time I would find something in a book I was reading, I would stick into it a little piece of paper – writing down some particular quote or noting what imaginative place it brought me to. I was reading and thinking, not certain where I was going with anything, and for most of the time I wasn't really sure what the lectures would even be about, and in fact that kind of helped me keep going. I'm a poet, and I'm the kind of poet who really doesn't know what he is doing when he is doing it. I make poems to find out what they say, not to make them say what I want. In fact, if I know where I'm going I rarely ever want to go there and would never actually end up there anyway. And for a while I thought the lecture should be about that – the experience of not knowing. Of moving inside the poem to find out what it will be, of letting the book be formed by that unknowing creation and not responding to it with any prepared set of needs and expectations.

For ten years I worked on a project – I was gathering quotations on birdsong. I started it with a friend but he drifted away almost immediately and I just kept doing it. I would find, in whatever it was I was reading, a caw or a call or an explanation of sound, and I would take that quote and copy it down. I'm not really sure why I was doing it. Birdsong seemed appealing and English. It felt at first, I think, like a kind of getting to know the poets I loved. The poets I loved loving birds. Dickinson through her window and Coleridge out in the hills. I think I found their joy and excitement joyous and exciting and wanted whatever that was – and that is basically what I got. That seemingly random and impromptu appearance of birds in our lives and how that was mimicked in my reading. I would be reading along and then there on the wire of some narrative a bird would land and start to sing. For a while this project was the most enjoyable thing – and I wasn't just enjoying myself, I was getting something done (sadly, that's *my* inner response to pleasure and leisure). There I was, no matter what I was reading, building some archive. To what end I really didn't know, but something was being made, something was growing. Then, after a while I would find myself waiting, not exactly skimming a book, but waiting for that moment I could take something from it.

Bird-watching is, in many ways, not about the birds but about their surroundings. It feels, while you are doing it, more like you are trying to act like a bird. There you are still, there your head moving quickly and anxiously in relation to some slight sound or movement. You stare at trees and bushes and the sky most of the time, and only rarely see another bird. The joy I think is being in the space they are in and imagining, in at least some way, you are attending to things they attend to, so that eventually when you do see the Elegant Trogon you feel a bit like the two of you have something in common. But with the books it began to feel too tactical. Like I was staring at them and only really interested in when the birds appeared. And so eventually I just stopped. I imagine there are plenty of reasons for tactical reading, for the kind of reading that has you getting something you already know you want, but that, for me, is the complete antithesis of art. So that if what I'm reading is art, treating it that way is not only undermining the work I'm looking at, it is making me less absorbent and less capable of big experience and feeling.

I remember I wanted to start the talk with a brief description of a scene in a film by Jacques Tati, where he (a French film actor, think a shy, well-mannered Charlie Chaplin) lackadaisically wanders through the market and up to his attic apartment by way of every possible stairwell and through every clothesline, doorway, and tight corner, getting there only to open a window, and what he was doing was opening the window so that a bit of light reflected off of it and went across the courtyard to land on a caged bird and once it hit the caged bird the caged bird started to sing. And he left the window open and adjusted for that reason. And it is not that finding what you have gone looking for is not pleasing, and it is not even that books being places you might do that is not a profound and exciting part of what they are, but just that, as a poet, I find the experience of the unknown is what excites me.

For me the closest I can come to telling seems to be sharing. The idea that one might get up and tell how things are the way they are or how things should be the way things should be seems, in a basic way, off from my experience of poetry. And it is so easy to imagine books as the solidifying process of an otherwise organic poetic experience – containing a mystery more than being a continually expanding one, but my experience tells me otherwise. And so a purposeful tactical writing feels odd. I want an investigative writing – experience and finding out as part of the speaking. Why would I say it if I think I know it? And once I do doesn't that make me want to question it? I thought, I know why I'd say it. I'd say it if you asked. And I thought one way to give this lecture would be simply to stand up here and have you all ask questions before I talked instead of after, and just answer questions until we were done. I could know a little about who you are, what you want and need instead of presenting some abstract relocation of my mind and experience for your benefit. And I thought, the thing about questions that appeals to me is basically how they express the location of the questioner. So that instead of talking into a big void of interest and disapproval, it would be more like talking with a friend. And I thought, really what I would do is open up for questions and whatever the first question was I would just try and answer that for an hour, using the placement and concerns of that individual to bounce off of as I talked, and as I did that the rest of you could locate us and the conversation's relation to your own thoughts and concerns.

There is this moment in Oscar Wilde's "The Decay of Lying" when Cyril asks Vivian if he is prepared to prove that it is not Art which imitates Nature, but Nature which imitates Art. To which Vivian replies, "My dear fellow, I am prepared to prove anything." I find it charming, not because it expresses some willingness to be false as much as an interest in the desire to engage any imaginative possibility. I find when I read him, no matter who is speaking and no matter if the work is fiction or not, I want to attribute the quote to the author. It's part of having the author there with you when you are reading. And I thought this, for a lecture on books, could be the central idea. That application of belief that the words are the author's, those senses feelings ideas attributed to that author and how simultaneously we feel we know the author and the author in a way knows us. I wanted to write about that experience of the book as an object one carries around and has with one – in one's life, during one's day and how the accompanying intimate experiences both of reading and of just holding and having and being companioned by can elevate that sense of proximity to the space of friendship and love. And how, simultaneously, whatever is living of the author can unfold and grow and change as it appears, be made as it appears.

The realness of these authors is only difficult when we think about it. How present they seem, equal at times to the flesh-and-blood ones that walk around. And I don't want it to be so simplistic. I don't believe that there the real authors are in full, presenting their spirits encapsulated in their perfect poems, but there maybe in the same way that a gesture might instantly activate in you an awareness of a person and express or create some actual presence of them. It is not as though they try or if they do, it is not as though their trying really brings them forth then after they are gone or while they are away, but almost their being in the presence of the poem seems to have left a residue of them for you to pick up when you spend time with the poem too, and what is that spending time but a kind of friendship.

Emerson, in his essay on friendship, talks about the ability to speak freely and to be heard that one finds comfortably in a friend, the disposal of inhibition in the face of acceptance. I identify that access of understanding as the central component of friendship. That it allows one to be oneself. So I think about the ways one might find oneself in friendship with poets, one might find companionship and understanding. Not that what they say makes you know them, but what they say makes you feel with them or heard by them. And it is that activatable companionship that the book as an object seems to propose. It can have, at times, while you are reading it, some aspect of the private letter, that expressive communication which presents from the outset a belief and interest in you.

There is something about the letter that gets us closer to the idea of the book. And poets, not uncommonly send their poems in letters and so the letter becomes some reconstruction or almost publication of what came before it, as the book might later. I think of Emily Dickinson. Resisting the harsh machinery of publication for the more intimate opportunities of private expression. She'd send a poem in a letter. And a poem might appear with as much or as little contextualization as was desired. And a poem became, in that moment of sending it, a physical thing, that they might have it in their lives too. That it traveled all the way to them. That they might have it to keep and save, to read and return to. I am sending you along this poem please do not share it with anyone or I am sending you along this poem please share with the whole family. I find in experiences of poems shared this way, that kernel of the book. Its making multiple. Its making possible. That it can travel and be and stay in other places, that while it may change the experience of the poem (as it has been private and with the poet alone), it may change that, but it doesn't necessarily diminish it. And for the receiver, for the reader, that experience of encounter is the becoming real of what wasn't there –

At half past Three, a single Bird
Unto a silent Sky
Propounded but a single term
Of cautious melody.

At Half past Four, Experiment
Had subjugated test
And lo, Her silver Principle
Supplanted all the rest.

At Half past Seven, Element
Nor Implement, be seen
And Place was where the Presence was
Circumference between.

And you could read a letter or a poem over and over again, reawakening the place and experiences of it. Its impossibilities and complexities, not that having that physical thing in front of you made it more controlled, just more proximate and alive –

At half past Three, a single Bird
Unto a silent Sky
Propounded but a single term
Of cautious melody.

At Half past Four, Experiment
Had subjugated test
And lo, Her silver Principle
Supplanted all the rest.

At Half past Seven, Element
Nor Implement, be seen
And Place was where the Presence was
Circumference between.

I wanted to do a lecture on that repeated quality we are allowed with recorded things. One might see something and return to it in their mind or try and conjure up a memory. Not making the poem complete, but accessible the way having a score for some music allows it to come to be repeatedly, actually. And the form, of its coming to be, retaining some obvious and physical presence. A presence that is reiterated each time it is returned to, but one that feels always in movement and always different, as a living thing you know to be a particular someone is different each time you encounter them. And this to me is maybe the core of the book. The poem as a physical object, that it may be and be returned to. Not that it is the same, but that it is capable of being again and again. That it is capable of being elsewhere and here. That it may be for one in some fashion similar to how it is for others, and that by being that way, there is a coming together of people.

In the beginning of one of his published journals, Jean Cocteau addresses his readers "the unknown friends enlisted by books" and imagines these friends as his "sole excuse for writing them." And reading that sort of validated my sense that though many of my friends may not have accepted my friendship in person (something about our personalities or selves in the way), there was something about their impulse not just to write but to make and share books that encouraged it later. And even his articulation, once shared, gets to be mine as well. I can take on his language and I can be comforted by the support our similarities imply.

There is a kind of book called a commonplace book. A commonplace book was to record and refine the ideas, anecdotes, and quotations that most forcefully made themselves a part of one's life. Those moments when a particular thought or expression answered the question one had struggled with or made a new question that landed in one's life with profound meaning. And because most of these were essentially quotes from others, it was important to have them in a place one could access. A place one could return to, not just to the feeling or even the idea, but to the language of it. That there was some concrete locale to all these articulations. And the book itself (and each one was a kind of companion) would accompany you in the world. These were all things one might return to in conversation or one might return to when speaking publicly. But, for the most part, a commonplace book was a private storehouse of those points of understanding that helped a thinking person move through their life. It was a lifelong endeavor, keeping such a book.

And one of the ideas for my lecture was simply – to take all the quotes and anecdotes and lay them down one after another, presenting, I guess, not only this span of thoughts and ideas, but the various and exceptional community of authors I met in books and the books I met them in. The quotes maintain some energy of the whole they were pulled from. The impossibilities of understanding their contexts giving the sense, the vastness of what is out there. So that even done without commentary, you (the listeners) would be left with some sort of display of ideas about books and some greater sense of one poet's experience of them as objects made, read, and found. And as I thought about it, I came to think that the constellation which would be more appealing would be that of the books themselves. This is, after all, a lecture about things, made things and the poem and how it finds its form in books and how the books form the experience of the poem and how the poetry passes through books as a way to find some stability in time, some stabilizing moments for them in the passing of times and lives. So it wasn't even the poems I wanted to get to but the constellation of forms. And I had a theory. My theory was this:

That interior to poems are all the various ends they will never meet. Inside them partially, those objects they did not become. The vibrant qualities of vibrant things are often that which they did not contain. The energies of intuitive choice seem to me to maintain in themselves at times the things they didn't choose – never actually having to say no, but just a following of impulses to find a way. So that at any point in a poem the next word can really be any word at all, and there is some energy of that constant possibility that I believe the poems maintain, even when they are done kind of making the words that are in them, and find themselves all written out. And maybe it goes further than that – that whatever possibilities there are for the poems, those possibilities are left open, are maintained in them as they proceed toward some eventual home, as, say, in a book. Books as form, as things, can be present in the poet, as a sort of end space or culmination or object, they can be basically absent from the poet, who, focused on the particular poem, is not compelled beyond whatever thingness it's got. Books can be an unlikely or uninteresting destination for poetry, or can be just one of many interesting destinations.

That to be a poet one might write forcefully toward some end, even if that end is not seen, understood, or recognized. The toward – maybe not even a poem – but then there they are sometimes – poems – pushing themselves toward some shared existence – say, in a book – not even seeing that yet. To be in that space toward, without the limitations of a goal. One can have in one's mind so many various books – that one can hold at times the deep and nuanced possibilities without being able to fix on any one. So that in you there is this multitude of formal possibility – changing – growing – presenting itself. So that as a poet, for me, the imagined library provides the landscape in which the things of what I make are made – and this feels formal – that one can hold in one's self these various formal results – and have in one no exact expectation –

So my theory was just – that the inside space of the poet could contain an imagined library, and that always-changing library could create a private cosmos of formal possibility. There is some aspect of writing poems that feels like feeling around, like a kind of echolocation, and it seems to me that books are made some way the same. Making them (from the very beginning) one has the sense of bouncing off and away from – various points recognized and solid, and in these bouncings off and away one finds a trajectory. So that while writing the poems (and when I say that I tend to think of ink and paper already), some sense of the physicality, the continued physicality, the eventual existence of the made solid place of the poems is present. That it can be to some extent present despite the maybe obvious fact that that writing, that the poetry of that moment, is unlikely to end up in a book or any other kind of public form. That the form of the book can be somehow related to that experience of making throughout, so that the closer to the forming of the book, the more maybe the physicality does its thing – repels or attracts – so that that thing that is to become the book (that thing that is to be the book) becomes in a way that has been happening all along. Not wittingly or knowingly, but has been present.

And I don't imagine that the central location of poetry is the book. Really, no, I imagine the central location of poetry is the world, the human world in which language is shared and kept in all sorts of ways. I think of the book as a constantly present and capable continuation of the acts of making poetry. And here I've gone and given you my theory without explaining a central part. Pages papers letters manuscripts alive inside of it. Experiences of the making mimicked in how it's made. To say it seems simplistic, but I will give it a try – there are all different kinds of books of poetry. That's it, there are all different kinds of books of poetry. Not that there are all different kinds of poetry that end up in books, which I think of as the more common sense of it. But that unlike most other forms of writing, poetry shoves, nudges, and creates its own spaces. And the only way I imagine to really express this, and the only way I imagine to express that cosmos of formal possibility, would be to describe hundreds of books, hundreds and hundreds of books. Not their poems, exactly, but their forms and the forms they came to have because of their poetry.

That, it seemed to me was the most obvious idea for a lecture on books. To display some part of my cosmos. What it is I bounce off of. And so I started to list and describe – books made privately and given as gifts, the book made from a diary that has the big present face of the author on its cover, the book of fragments gathered by one's family, the pink-paged book with its musical notations, or the enormous book that expresses with its size the nature and depth, the vastness of its endeavor. The thin narrow book with its thin narrow poems. But the more I started to list and describe the more abstract they seemed, which makes sense. When I'm not thinking about them, that's exactly what they are – abstract presence of meaningful things. But here we are actually thinking and talking about them, so that I want to go deeper, I want to describe them more. The form of the book built around itself, so that when I'm describing a book of short fragmentary poems, I can say there they are on their big white pages, the space around them expressing time or making quiet, and the quiet and time around them elevating them in some way or making the ink and presence of words more solid, and the experience of that page after page, or the touch of the paper when you've been looking mostly at it – the physical qualities of sparseness.

And even that didn't work, look how removed from its person it is. What poems are they, who is this author, where is this book?

So I guess we've come all the way around, and maybe the only way to do this is not to describe that imagined cosmos but to introduce a single point in it. Describe a single book. Describe the life of a single book. Over here the tree growing that the paper will come from and over here the poetry starting to form in the person or in the family of the person as the person is forming, and then the poems over time happening and finding their form while the sources of need and want around the poet grow, drawing the poem out into the public world and the ways that object comes to be and then following just one of them, just one book out to its recipient, and the life that person has with it, reading it, scribbling in its margins, speaking its poems aloud or leaving it quietly on the shelf.

Yes, I thought, that's the lecture I should give.

ACKNOWLEDGMENTS

The Bagley Wright Lecture Series on Poetry supports contemporary poets as they explore in-depth their own thinking on poetry and poetics, and give a series of lectures resulting from these investigations.

"On Books" (previously titled "On the Porous Experience of the Book in Physical and Imagined Space") was given at the Woodberry Room at Harvard University, October 16, 2014. "Friendship, Porousness, and the Intimate Experience of Poetry" was given at the Poetry Foundation, Chicago, IL, on May 22, 2014, and "The Friend, the Stranger, and the Intimate Experience of Poetry" at Seattle Arts and Lectures in Seattle, WA, on May 29, 2014. Thank you to Christina Davis at Harvard, Stephen Young at the Poetry Foundation, Rebecca Hoogs at Seattle Arts and Lectures, and their respective staffs, for welcoming the Bagley Wright Lecture Series into their programming, and for collaborating on scheduling, promoting, introducing, and recording these events. The Series would be impossible without such partners.

Excerpts from *The Journal of John Wieners Is To Be Called 707 Scott Street for Billie Holiday 1959* appear courtesy of the Estate of John Wieners. Paul Blackburn entries are excerpted from *The Journals* (Black Sparrow, 1975). Excerpts from "The Verse Record of My Peonies," *Japanese Poetic Diaries: Selected and Translated, with an Introduction*, by Earl Roy Miner, © 1969 by the Regents of the University of California. Used with permission. Excerpt from *Romaji Diary and Sad Toys* by Takuboku Ishikawa, © 1985 by Tuttle Publishing, appears with permission. Excerpt from *The Collected Essays of Robert Creeley* by Robert Creeley, © 1989 by University of California Press, appears with permission of University of California Press. "Gone Now" by Susie Timmons (from *Superior Packets*, © 2015) appears with permission of the author and Wave Books. Brathwaite, Kamau. THE ZEA MEXICAN DIARY. © 1993 by the Regents of the University of Wisconsin System. Reprinted courtesy of the University of Wisconsin Press. "XXXIII" reprinted from *Stephen Jonas, Selected Poems* by Stephen Jonas, © 1994 by Talisman House, appears with permission of the Estate of Stephen Jonas. Poems from *The Collected Poems of Larry Eigner* by Larry Eigner, © 2010 by Stanford University Press, appear with permission. "[Easy to Love]" reprinted from *Elise Cowen: Poems and Fragments* by Elise Cowen, © 2014 by Ahsahta Press, appears with permission of Jonathan R. Nash. Poems from *About Now: Collected Poems* (National Poetry Foundation, 2007) appear with permission of the Estate of Joanne Kyger. Lew Welch, "[I Saw Myself]" from *Ring of Bone: Collected Poems 1950–1971*. Copyright © 1979 by Donald Allen. Reprinted with the permission of The Permissions Company, Inc., on behalf of City Lights Books, www.citylights.com. "The Language" from *The Collected Poems of Robert Creeley, 1945–1975* by Robert Creeley, © 2006 by University of California Press, appears with permission of University of California Press. "An Irregular Ode" from *The Collected Poems of Philip Whalen* © 2007 by Brandeis University Press. Published by Wesleyan University Press. Used by permission of Wesleyan University Press and the Estate of Philip Whalen. Dickinson poem is reprinted by permission of the publishers from *The Poems of Emily Dickinson: Reading Edition*, edited by Ralph W. Franklin, Cambridge, Mass.: The Belknap Press of Harvard University Press, Copyright © 1998, 1999 by the President and Fellows of Harvard College. Copyright © 1951, 1955 by the President and Fellows of Harvard College. Copyright © renewed 1979, 1983 by the President and Fellows of Harvard College. Copyright © 1914, 1918, 1919, 1924, 1929, 1930, 1932, 1935, 1937, 1942 by Martha Dickinson Bianchi. Copyright © 1952, 1957, 1958, 1963, 1965 by Mary L. Hampson.

NOTE FROM THE AUTHOR

I would like to thank the Bagley Wright Lecture Series, and in particular Charlie Wright and Matthew Zapruder for inviting me to give these talks and for their support and enthusiasm throughout the process, as well as Ellen Welcker for her close attention as they were being given and to the resulting manuscripts. I would like to thank Heidi Broadhead for her thoughtful engagement with the lectures as they went through many edits, and for her tireless work bringing the process to fruition. Throughout the course of writing and giving these it became clear that whatever I was talking about, I was in some way talking about friendship, and that at the core of the various experiences and recognitions, I found present the voices and selves of individuals I have been close to over the years. I am thankful for those friendships and I am thankful for the many who took the time to read, listen, and respond – in particular Anthony, Gregory, Matt, Melanie, and Peter.

Both the nature of, and ideas considered within, these talks feel in different ways deeply indebted to both Alejandro de Acosta and James Walsh – for years of correspondence and conversation, out of which so much of this grew.